Thank you for your
contributions to
Old Dominion University

M Lee Manning

Teaching Learners At-Risk

Teaching Learners At-Risk

M. Lee Manning
Old Dominion University

Leroy G. Baruth
Appalachian State University

Christopher-Gordon Publishers, Inc.
Norwood, Massachusetts

Copyright Acknowledgments

Every effort has been made to contact copyright holders for permission to reproduce borrowed material where necessary. We apologize for any oversights and would be happy to rectify them in future printings.

Excerpt from Reiff, J. (1997) Multiple Intelligences, Culture, and equitable Learning. *Childhood Education, 73*(5), 301–304.

Christopher-Gordon Publishers, Inc.
1502 Providence Highway, Suite 12
Norwood, MA 02062
800-934-8322

Printed in the United States of America

10 9 8 7 6 5 4 3 2 1   05 04 03 02 01 00

Library of Congress Catalog Card Number: 99-076804
ISBN: 1929024-15-0

Dedication

To Marianne, for her encouragement and support,
and to teachers and administrators who work daily
to teach, guide, help, and nurture K–8 learners at-risk.
—MLM

To Carmella, for her distinguished career in many
facets of education, especially the preparation of
the teachers of tomorrow.
—LGB

Table of Contents

Detailed Table of Contents

Chapter 5: Classroom Management Techniques and Strategies

Preface

K–8 Learners At-Risk

Many indicators suggest K–8 children are at-risk: underachievers, substance abuse, physical aggression toward peers and teachers, inappropriate sexual behavior, lack of respect for others and their rights, and violence perceived as a viable means of solving problems. Learners at-risk can be helped when elementary and middle school educators plan educational experiences that address specific at-risk conditions and behaviors. In fact, we think learners at-risk face a promising future—learners at-risk can be reliably identified, characteristics of effective programs can be listed, teaching strategies can be suggested, the need for alternative learning environments is clear, and educators realize the importance of involving parents and families in the education of learners at-risk. Undoubtedly, this improved knowledge base and the increasing number of elementary and middle school educators committed to helping learners at-risk suggest these learners will have a bright and promising future.

Our Reasons for Writing "Teaching Learners At-Risk"

We have worked for many years with learners at-risk in a number of capacities: classroom teachers, counselors, consultants, researchers and writers, and grant-writers. Also, we have worked collaboratively with many teachers of learners at-risk as they worked to address the students' needs. We understand the challenges facing both learners and educators as well as share their hopes that learners' at-risk conditions and behaviors will be addressed. Our specific reasons for writing *Teaching Learners At-Risk* include:

1. We think K–8 learners can and should be provided with educational experiences that will make a difference in their lives and that address specific at-risk conditions and behaviors.
2. We think educational efforts should be comprehensive, that is, identifying learners at-risk, planning effective at-risk programs, deciding appropriate instruction, planning alternative learning environments, implementing classroom management, and involving parents and families.

3. We have many first-hand experiences with learners at-risk and want to share with others, motivate and inspire, and improve the lives of learners at-risk as well as their educators.

The Organization of "Teaching Learners At-Risk"

Teaching Learners At-Risk is divided into six chapters:

Chapter 1. Identification of Learners At-Risk focuses on characteristics that suggest the possibility of students being placed at-risk.

Chapter 2. Characteristics of Effective At-Risk Programs suggests essential characteristics such as providing comprehensive efforts; promoting self-esteem; emphasizing high expectations; teaching social skills; insisting teachers and learners agree on educational experiences; involving parents and families; and focusing on the relationship between motivation and success.

Chapter 3. Methods, Strategies, and Assessment focuses on instructional methods and strategies such as individualized instruction, cooperative learning, learning styles, multiple intelligences, alternatives to ability grouping and tracking, and appropriate assessment.

Chapter 4. Alternative Learning Environments is based upon the belief that many children at-risk might be unable to succeed in regular classroom settings, but can be quite successful in alternative learning environments with less competition, an emphasis on the positive, and smaller classes grouped heterogeneously.

Chapter 5. Classroom Management Techniques and Strategies suggests that management includes two separate yet overlapping entities, i.e., educators' efforts to manage actual behavior management of students and educators' teaching and organizational behaviors.

Chapter 6. Parents and Families focuses on understanding parents' and families' educational efforts such as reasons for including parents of learners at-risk, how conferences can be most effective, and ways to involve parents and families.

Special Features and Pedagogical Aids

Teaching Learners At-Risk includes several pedagogical features that we think readers will find helpful:

- Chapter Objectives—Chapter objectives serve as an advance organizer and provide readers with a look at the topics to be explored and what they should be able to do after reading and thinking about the chapter.
- Case Studies—Case Studies show how educators handled specific problems dealing with learners at-risk.
- Research and Classroom Practice—This pedagogical aid highlights current research and how educators of K–8 learners at-risk have implemented or might implement the research.

- Methods and Strategies—This feature is interspersed throughout all chapters and offers practical suggestions to readers.
- For Additional Information—Several annotated suggested readings and internet sites provide readers with sources of additional information.

Our Appreciation to Others

We want to offer our appreciation to the many K–8 teachers of learners at-risk who have told us of their challenges and joys and who have shared their suggestions for helping learners at-risk. These teachers make a difference in the lives of children—we appreciate both their efforts to help children at-risk as well as their suggestions for making *Teaching Learners At-Risk* readable and practical.

We also want to thank Dr. Katherine Bucher of Old Dominion University for her assistance. She has tirelessly helped us find research and references. We appreciate her sharing both her time and expertise.

Our appreciation is extended to the reviewers: Sarah Jordan, Leslie Roberts, and Sandra Fehr, and to our editor at Christopher-Gordon: Susanne Canavan.

—MLM
Old Dominion University

—LGB
Appalachian State University

Chapter 1	# Identification of Learners At-Risk

Overview

A number of at-risk conditions and behaviors affect elementary and middle school students. Elementary and middle school educators benefit from understanding what places students at-risk as well as knowing appropriate identification devices. Two students might share similar at-risk characteristics, yet one might be at-risk while the other is not. Plus, all learners probably demonstrate at-risk characteristics at some time and, in fact, some school practices might actually contribute to at-risk conditions and behaviors. Elementary and middle school educators have a professional responsibility to understand the various at-risk conditions and behaviors and to provide appropriate educational experiences.

Chapter Objectives

After reading and thinking about this chapter on identification of learners at-risk, the reader should be able to:

1. Define at-risk conditions and behaviors and recognize the importance of understanding those factors that place elementary and middle school learners at-risk.

2. Explain how all learners might sometimes be at-risk and how some learners might be at-risk because they are average.

3. List several factors that can contribute to learners being at-risk.

4. Suggest how to determine when a learner is or is not at-risk and the importance of using considerable caution in the process to identify learners at-risk.

5. Discuss selected at-risk conditions and behaviors such as lower achievers and special needs; poverty and lower socioeconomic conditions; health and eating disorders; drug, alcohol, and tobacco use; physical and psychological violence; and peer pressure.

6. Suggest ways to identify learners that might be placed at-risk.
7. Explain how school practices and policies may actually place learners at-risk.

At-Risk Conditions and Behaviors in K–8 Learners

Defining At-Risk Conditions and Behaviors

The term, "at-risk," varies among educators and situations. For the purpose of *Teaching Learners At-Risk*, we offer a broad definition of at-risk as "those conditions and behaviors that limit or have the potential to limit learners' academic achievement, socialization, and physical and mental health." Admittedly, this definition is broad; however, we think a broader definition will be more educationally beneficial than a narrower or more specific one. Although some overlap exists, we see conditions as disabilities, socioeconomic status, health problems, school performance, peer relations, self-esteem, family instability, and lack of parental support. Similarly, we view behaviors as substance abuse, attempted suicides, and sexual activity. In some ways students might have little control over their conditions—some of the students we have taught have been exceedingly poor. Behaviors, on the other hand, might be more by choice, although peer pressure to engage in risky behaviors often leaves little room for rational choices.

All Learners Being At-Risk at Sometime

We once spoke with a thirteen-year-old girl about the various at-risk conditions affecting some learners in her age group. She perceptively responded, "*All* learners are at-risk at some time!" This young girl had a keen understanding of learners that educators often overlook. All learners can be at-risk at various points in their lives and not be at-risk at others. The following quote illustrates the diversity among learners at-risk:

> At-risk youth cannot be stereotyped by color, age, economic level, or family situation. They belong to all races. They include infants, children, and teens. They come from two-parent and single-parent families, some rich, some poor. Some at-risk youth live in the suburbs, others on farms and in cities (National Catholic Education Association 1993, p. 4).

The risk of being average

Some educators working to challenge brighter students and reacting to disorderly students sometimes overlook average learners. Clearly, students of all ages and abilities can be at-risk when teachers focus time and energy only on bright high-achievers and on misbehaving students. Average learners can be at-risk and their conditions might grow more acute when educators ignore or fail to recognize danger signs (Wylie, 1992; Helge, 1990).

Methods and Strategies 1.1 suggests several ways K–8 educators can be sure they consider all students.

Methods and Strategies 1.1: Considering Average Students

Educators determining whether average students are at-risk can be on the lookout for several factors such as family stability, school performance, peer relations, participation in school activities, overall self-esteem, depression, suicide attempts, child abuse, alcoholic parents, migrant, being sexually active, and changes in personal health (Wylie, 1992; Helge, 1990).

The Need to Consider Developmental Perspectives of Learners At-Risk

At-risk conditions and behaviors vary with age and development. Kindergarten and lower-elementary children might experience problems with being away from home or being overly shy, while middle school learners might be more inclined to experiment with sexual activity and engage in substance abuse. In fact, development often places students at-risk; i.e., early or late development can take a considerable toll. Learners, passing through the various developmental stages, face a number of tasks and challenges which potentially can place them at-risk. Older elementary and middle school students might experience at-risk conditions when forming new friendships, developing unfamiliar physical skills, growing toward independence, and developing appropriate sex roles. A learner experiencing difficulty making friends or feeling awkward in physical education class can also experience a low self-esteem which can lead to at-risk behaviors to compensate for feelings of frustration and inadequacies. Considering *individual* learners is the only effective way to determine a student's propensity to being at-risk.

Factors That Place Children At-Risk

Table 1.1 lists selected factors that can contribute to learners being at-risk. It is important to note that Frymier, Barber, Carriedo, Denton, Gansneder, Johnson-Lewis, and Robertson, (1992) had a more exhaustive list, but we selected the factors in table 1.1 because they are most applicable to K–8 learners.

Determining when a learner is or is not at-risk.

One essential key to successful teaching of learners at-risk is to use caution in determining who is and who is not at-risk. For example, caution should be used to avoid placing all low socioeconomic learners at-risk; while being poor can be an at-risk condition, many students from socioeconomically poor backgrounds demonstrate positive behavior and achievement in school. Likewise, students should not be placed at-risk on the basis of their cultural backgrounds. To place a boy at-risk because he is from a differing cultural background is a serious mistake and shows a lack of educational judgement. Generalizations and

Table 1.1—Factors Placing Students At-Risk

- Attempted suicide during the past year.
- Engaged in substance abuse.
- Harbors a negative self-esteem.
- Was pregnant during the past year.
- Was expelled from school during the past year.
- Have parents with negative attitudes toward school.
- Has brothers or sisters who are school dropouts.
- Was sexually or physically abused.
- Failed two subjects during the last year.
- Was absent from school more than twenty days last year.
- Has an alcoholic parent.
- Has been previously retained in a grade.
- Has a parent who has attempted suicide.
- Scored below the 20th percentile on standardized test.
- Attended more than three schools during the last five years.
- Had average grades below a "C" last school year.
- Had parents who divorced or separated last year.
- Has father or mother who is unemployed, unskilled laborer.
- Had mother or father to die during previous year.
- Has been selected for special education class.
- Speaks a native language other than English.
- Lives in urban, inner city.
- Has only the mother living at home.
- Is year older than other students in the same grade.
- Has mother who was high school dropout.
- Has father who lost his job during the last year.
- Was dropped from an athletic team during the last year.
- Experienced a serious illness or accident.

Developed from: Frymier, J., Barber, L., Carriedo, R., Denton, W., Gansneder, B., Johnson-Lewis, S., & Robertson, N. (1992). *Growing up is risky business, and schools are not to blame.* Final report, Phi Delta Kappa study of students at-risk, vol. 1 (Bloomington, IN: Phi Delta Kappa).

stereotypes should never be used to place a student at-risk regardless of her or his economic status or cultural heritage. Elementary and middle school teachers should use only objective and accurate information such as checklists of identifying characteristics and teacher and parent referral, just to name selected examples.

Methods and Strategies 1.2 suggests educators ask several questions to determine whether a student is actually at-risk.

✔ Methods and Strategies 1.2: Determining Whether a Student is Actually At-Risk

1. Does the condition (i.e., socioeconomic status) affect the learner's academic achievement, behavior, motivation, or social standing in the class?
2. Are there indications the learner's self-esteem is hurt due to the condition?
3. Do the parents feel the condition hurts their son's or daughter's chances of succeeding in school?
4. Does the learner appear to experience undue stress?
5. Does the learner feel he or she is at-risk or that "something is wrong?"

Also, people, including K–8 educators, sometimes blame young people for being at-risk. "Brought it on himself," we heard one teacher say. Another said, "She is doing it to herself." We want to emphasize the importance of not blaming students for their predicaments. In almost all cases, some causal factor exists—the factor does not excuse the behavior, but it does deserve understanding. In many situations, we think blaming the victim has the potential for placing the learner at even greater risk. For example, overeaters' or anorexics' at-risk conditions might grow more acute when blamed for their eating disorders. Second, disturbing consequences can follow when learners living in poverty receive blame for their socioeconomic conditions.

Identification of Selected At-Risk Conditions and Behaviors

While naming all at-risk conditions and behaviors is an impossible task, we have chosen conditions and behaviors that we think will challenge educators in today's elementary and middle schools.

Lower Achievers and Special Needs

Underachievement or failing to achieve at one's potential poses a common problem for both learners at-risk and their educators. The numbers of students falling one or more grade levels behind in school provide disturbing and convincing evidence that educators should identify lower achievers at the earliest possible time. The consequences of lower achievement or failing to achieve at one's potential can have serious consequences on cognitive development as well as learners' motivation and self-esteem.

One failure often leads to additional failures or the expectation of failing. The issue of lower achievement is especially serious because learners need to develop positive beliefs in their ability to meet personal and school expectations. Once teachers label K–8 learners as lower achievers, the task of catching-up and achieving at expected levels becomes difficult. In fact, once students begin functioning below grade level, the tendency to fall further behind increases with each additional grade. Also, lower achievement results in an increased likelihood of eventually dropping out of school altogether.

Chapter 5 looks at special needs (such as learning disabilities, emotionally disturbed, attention deficit hyperactive disorder, and limited English proficiency) students in more detail; however, at this point table 1.2 shows significant numbers exist to warrant teachers' attention.

Table 1.2—Children With Disabilities 1996	
Disabilities	**Percent Distribution**
Specific learning disabilities	51.3
Speech or language impairments	20.3
Mental retardation	11.3
Serious emotional disturbance	8.7
Hearing impairments	1.3
Orthopedic impairments	1.2
Other health impairments	2.6
Visual impairments	0.5
Multiple disabilities	1.8
Autism	0.6
Traumatic brain injury	0.2

Source: U.S. Bureau of the Census. (1998). *Statistical abstracts of the United States 1998.* 118th edition, Washington, DC: Government Printing Office.

Characteristics suggesting learners might be at-risk of being lower achievers include:

1. Failing to complete homework or class assignments.
2. Showing little or no motivation or goal-oriented behaviors.
3. Achieving one or more grade levels behind.

4. Showing acceptable achievement, and then, showing below average achievement.
5. Speaking of not caring or the desire to drop out of school upon reaching the legal age.

Methods and Strategies 1.3 looks at several programs designed to address the needs of students with special needs.

Methods and Strategies 1.3: Identifying Special Programs

After first determining the specific challenges faced by students with special needs, educators can look toward several specialized programs such as bilingual education, English as a second language, remedial reading, remedial mathematics, programs for the disabled, programs for the gifted and talented, diagnostic and prescriptive programs, and extended day programs. Case Study 1.1 looks at how a teacher helped a twelve year old boy succeed academically.

Case Study 1.1: Helping a Student Academically At-Risk

Chip was a twelve year old who was academically at-risk. At the first of the year, Chip said, "Mr. Bennett, I am going to fail spelling this year—might make a D, but no higher. Always have. My mother and father can't spell either. I will make a D or F." Mr. Bennett checked Chip's permanent records and he was right— he had always made a D or F. Mr. Bennett said, "Chip, I will work with you to help you get a higher grade." That year, after much work, high expectations, encouragement, and study, Chip earned a C for the year. To some students in the class, a C would have been considered failure, but Chip felt like a success.

Mr. Bennett challenged Chip—he conveyed high expectations, he maximized the momentum, he encouraged and convinced, and he never let Chip's self-doubt last long. Was he as successful with all students in the class? No, but he never quit trying; however, emphasizing academic achievement, fostering self-esteem, and challenging work and momentum were keys to success for many.

Poverty and Lower Socioeconomic Conditions

The number of people living in poverty continues to be startling: Over 3.6 million people (13.7%) lived below the poverty level in 1996 and nearly five million (18.5%) lived below 125% of poverty level (U.S. Bureau of the Census, 1998). Poverty and its effects can be numerous—lack of ambition, lower academic achievement, poor health, lower self-esteem, and failure to achieve feelings of being able to influence one's world. However, educators should use caution to avoid labeling all learners experiencing poverty. First, a learner living in poverty for a short time (perhaps due to the mother or the father being temporarily unemployed) may not be at-risk or may be at-risk for only a short period of time. Second, not all learners living in poverty experience at-risk conditions. While one can safely assume that poverty contributes to learners being at-risk, some learners may overcome the ill effects of poverty and work themselves out of what would have been an at-risk condition. Likewise, a strong sense of family or commitment to overcoming adversity has the potential for outweighing the effects of poverty.

Ways to identify learners who might be at-risk due to poverty and lower socioeconomic conditions include:

1. Hunger, fatigue, homelessness, and excessive body odors.
2. Lack of care such as personal hygiene and health.
3. Lack of money to pay for school-related experiences.
4. Lives with one parent who cannot earn sufficient money for the necessities of life.
5. Lack of motivation and a seemingly fatalistic perspective toward life and toward one's future.

Alcohol, Drugs, and Tobacco

Alcohol, drug, and tobacco use represent major health problems which either make older elementary learners at-risk or worsen their chances of overcoming at-risk conditions. A parallel problem results: Alcohol, drug, and tobacco can contribute to other at-risk tendencies or behaviors such as teenage pregnancy, health problems, or eventual withdrawal from school. Whether caused by wanting to act grownup or conforming to societal and peer expectations, the tobacco, alcohol, and drug problem without doubt poses serious at-risk threats. Another disturbing problem is the younger ages at which children begin to experiment with dangerous substances.

The Census Bureau reported in 1996 that children 12–17 years reported the following drug use: Marijuana and hashish (16.2%), alcohol (38.8%), and cigarettes (36.3%) (U.S. Bureau of the Census, 1998).

The effects of alcohol, drugs, and tobacco can be devastating on learners' developing physical, psychosocial, and cognitive growth which can be harmed and perhaps permanently damaged. Physical growth can be stunted; psychosocially, learners might withdraw or grow dependent on alcohol; and cognitively, thought processes might be slowed or delayed. Of course, more serious harm might occur such as brain damage or even death.

Methods and Strategies 1.4 suggests several ways educators can teach about the dangers of alcohol, drugs, and tobacco.

✔ ## Methods and Strategies 1.4:
Ways to Address Alcohol, Drug, and Tobacco Use

Educators may address the dangers of alcohol, drugs, and tobacco in several ways:

- Just Say No programs.
- Comprehensive drug and alcohol counseling at school.
- Alcoholics and Narcotics Anonymous programs (school-based and designed for young people).
- Drug-Free programs that are government funded.
- Life skills training (especially for later elementary and middle school learners).
- Teachers and counselors working collaboratively.
- Professional inservice training for all educators working in the school.

Teenage Pregnancy and Sexually Transmitted Diseases

Statistics on sexual activity, pregnancies, and abortions indicate that young learners increasingly participate in at-risk behaviors. Barth, Middleton, and Wagman (1989) summarized that teenage pregnancy remains the major reason for students leaving school; by the age of 15, 6.6% of females and 17.5% of male teenagers have had intercourse; sexually active adolescents do not use contraception consistently or effectively, and almost 20% of all teens have an unintended pregnancy. Although these numbers probably pertain more to high school students, many learners likely begin sexual activity during the later elementary and middle school years.

Unlike many of the other risks that young people face, the risks associated with AIDS represent a life-or-death matter. Among persons of all ages in the United States, HIV infection/AIDS is the eighth leading cause of death. The number of AIDS cases increases approximately 3% each year. Young peoples' inexperience and lack of knowledge make them a particularly vulnerable group (Rosenberg, Biggar, & Goedert, 1994). During 1997, 306 cases of AIDS were reported for children under 5 years old, and 145 cases between the ages of 5 and 12 (U.S. Bureau of the Census, 1998).

Although usually not as deadly, sexually transmitted diseases (STDS) pose a risk for young people. Young people, often curious about sexual activity and sometimes prone to sexual experimentation, can contract a STD which can impede their development and overall health. Topics about STDS can be discussed in health classes, guidance programs, and exploratory programs. The school nurse and guidance counselor can also play important roles in helping learners learn about STDS.

Health and Eating Disorders

Compared to adults, most K–8 learners generally suffer fewer illnesses commonly associated with aging. In 1995, major illnesses among children under 5 years old included infections, common colds, influenza, digestive system problems, and injuries. Major causes of death in 1 to 14 year olds include congenital abnormalities, cancer, heart disease, HIV infections, pneumonia and influenza, and cerebrovascular diseases. In 1995, days missed from school due to illness were 4.2 for males and 4.9 for females (U.S. Bureau of the Census, 1998). Some learners experience acute health conditions which possibly can place them at-risk. The Census Bureau reports acute health conditions for children age 5 to 17 years include infective and parasitic conditions, common colds, influenza, digestive system problems, and injuries (U.S. Bureau of the Census, 1998). (The Census Bureau does not report data just for K–8 learners.)

Some older elementary and middle school students experience an obsession with thinness. Anorexia nervosa, a psychological and physical disturbance, is when a person starves herself (females makeup 95% of anorexics), exercises compulsively, and develops an unrealistic view of her body. Bulimia, another closely related eating disorder, differs from anorexia nervosa. Whereas the anorexic aims to lose weight by not eating, the bulimic tries to eat without gaining weight. The bulimic experiences eating sprees or binges, yet considers the eating pattern abnormal. The young person fears not being able to stop eating and experiences a depressed mood and self-disparaging thoughts after eating binges. Then, the person self-induces vomiting so weight will not be gained. Complex causes and treatment underlay these disorders, and between 10% and 20% of youngsters who do not receive professional help die of starvation and its consequences (Seifert & Hoffnung, 1991).

Depression, a contemporary and common problem, often affects children. Symptoms may include change in appetite or weight, sleep disturbances, psychomotor problems, loss of interest in usual activities, loss of energy, feelings of worthlessness or excessive guilt, complaints of difficulty to concentrate, and thoughts of death or suicide. Depression, however, may not always be termed as such and may be cited as learning disabilities, hyperactivity, school phobia, somatic complaints, and conduct disorders.

Several consequences result from K–8 learners being at-risk due to health reasons. First, believing one will be perpetually healthy can result in one not taking reasonable care of the body or taking unnecessary risks which can result in injuries or death. Second, inadequate nutrition can interfere with a learners' ability to concentrate at school and to engage in peer-related activities. Third, an obsession with thinness can result in serious health problems and even death.

Signs suggesting learners may be at-risk of health and eating disorders include:
1.   Overweight for height and age.
2.   Poor body image.
3.   Compulsive and obsessive exercising.
4.   Depression and sadness.
5   Loneliness and withdrawal.

6. Evidence of a sexually transmitted disease.
7. Absences from school indicating health problems.
8. Changes in appetite and weight.
9. One or more illnesses and/or diseases.
10. Evidence of substance use (drugs, alcohol, and tobacco).

Peer Pressure

Peers represent a powerful and often underestimated source of influence in the social, academic, and overall development and actual behavior and attitudes of K–8 learners. The number of boys and girls engaging in at-risk behaviors such as smoking, alcohol use, and sexual activity provides evidence of how peers can influence another's attitudes and behaviors. In fact, the peer group can become the primary reference for behavior, values, and decision-making.

Educators need to accept the fact that peer pressure will always influence youngsters' behavior, attire, and speech. Additionally, educators should remember that their attempts to compete with peers are usually difficult at best. While peer pressure remains a vital part of the socialization process, a healthy self-concept still serves as the best antidote to negative peer pressure. For example, a director of a drug prevention program told us that a healthy self-concept was one of the most effective means of preventing and combating drug abuse. A confident and successful student who feels good about the "self," the school, and the home might be less likely to "go along with the crowd"; however, the student at-risk, who may already feel unsuccessful and unconfident, might be even more at-risk of giving in to peers in an attempt to feel accepted or a part of the group.

It should be remembered, though, that some peer pressure can be positive; perceptive educators readily recognize that peer pressure can be used to influence positive behavior. For example, peer pressure can be used to encourage academic achievement and to promote socially acceptable behaviors. The educator's task will be to decide how most effectively to lessen the influence of negative peer pressure (i.e., pressure to engage in at-risk behaviors) and also how to most effectively use peer pressure to encourage desirable behaviors (e.g., working cooperatively toward a group goal).

Signs suggesting a learner might succumb to peer pressure include:

1. Changing one's dress, mannerisms, and behaviors to conform to peer expectations.
2. Joining a gang or showing allegiance to "problem" students.
3. Showing an obvious tendency to misbehave or engage in risky behaviors.
4. Changing one's "hours"—such as coming to school late or failing to meet parent's curfews.
5. Showing a decline in academic achievement "to be more like friends and peers."

6. Having an inordinate desire to be liked and to gain others' approval.

Methods and Strategies 1.5 suggests several ways to lessen the influence of negative peer pressure.

Methods and Strategies 1.5:
Combatting Negative Peer Pressure

1. Provide self-esteem exercises where students can develop a realistic appraisal of their abilities and self-worth.
2. Provide collaborative learning groups that "mix" peers, so students at risk of peer pressure will not always work with the students who encourage at-risk behaviors.
3. Help learners have successful school experiences, so they might not see a need to gain attention in negative ways.
4. Teach collaboration and a sense of cooperation, so students will not feel a need to join a gang or become involved in gang activity.
5. Provide programs (e.g., gang prevention, substance abuse, and conflict resolution) that might assist students in either avoiding or dealing with peer pressure.

Physical and Psychological Violence

Incidents of aggression and violence increase annually at alarming rates in our schools. The U.S. Department of Justice reports three million crimes—or about 11% of all crimes, occur each year in public schools (Sautter, 1995). Teenagers more frequently are victims of crime than any other age group; and, a quarter of the crimes committed against them occur in or near schools. Most school violence consists of less extreme acts such as bullying, verbal and physical threats, shoving, and fist fights. Male students are three times more likely than females to be involved in aggression (Carnegie Council on Adolescent Development, 1989). While the U.S. Census reports do not differentiate between firearms deaths in and out of school, disturbing numbers still prevail. In 1995, among 5 to 14 year olds, 2,500 White students and 5,500 African American students died from firearms, either as accidents or homicides (U.S. Bureau of the Census, 1998). Rather than one isolated cause for aggression, research suggests that substance abuse, victimization, marital discord/spouse abuse, depression, exposure to violence in the mass media, and extreme poverty all play a role (Gable, 1994).

Children who witness violence are affected emotionally and cognitively. The foundation of healthy development—a sense of security and predictability—is threatened. Also, exposure to violence can result in post-traumatic stress disorders such as reexperiencing the event in play enactment or frequent nightmares, withdrawal or passivity, temporary loss of developmental skills, increased irritability, hypervigilance and hyperaggression, and decreased concentration (Jackson, 1999).

Ways to identify learners placed at-risk of physical and psychological violence include learners:

1. Being physically harmed (such as a fight) or psychologically harmed (such as teasing, bullying, or taunting).
2. Attending school where students threaten others with guns or knives.
3. Being unable to explain bruises, cuts, and abrasions.
4. Being verbally abused—threatened or yelled at—by teachers and administrators.
5. Experiencing a rapid loss of self-esteem.
6. Exhibiting a sudden desire to stay home from school.
7. Confiding with teachers they are afraid to attend school.

Methods and Strategies 1.6 suggests ways to address physical and psychological violence.

Methods and Strategies 1.6:
Addressing Physical Violence

1. Maintain a vigilant lookout for weapons of any kind—these might include "homemade" or purchased weapons.
2. Look for students who feel isolated, perhaps loners who feel alienated or left out of the mainstream of the school.
3. Provide conflict resolution for all students, so they can learn ways to deal with conflicts other than resorting to violence.
4. Involve parents and community members in the identification of possibly violent students as well as their potential victims.

Research and Classroom Practice 1.1 suggests how educators can create a climate of healing in a violent society.

Research and Classroom Practice 1.1:
Creating a Climate of Healing in a Violent Society

Contending that violence affects young children, Beverly Roberson Jackson (1999) called for early childhood professionals to take action to make child care centers and schools a safe haven. Specifically, she called for early care and education settings to 1) provide a safe haven for children who have witnessed or experienced violence; 2) foster relationships with individual children and their home and community; and 3) encourage the development of critical skills that lead to moral development.

Jackson (1999) maintained a climate of healing can be worked toward in several ways:

1. Build worthwhile relationships with parents—support parents in their effort to create a calm, secure, and safe environment; meet with families to plan ways to address violence in children's lives; and reassure parents their input is genuinely valued.

2. Provide a safe and secure learning environment—provide unhurried attention by a number of staff able to concentrate on the needs of individual children; provide responsive caregiving in which long-term relationships develop; and provide a safe and caring environment in which children are assured that they will be safe and protected—not bullied or taunted in the classroom or on the playground.

Source: Jackson, B. R. (1999). Creating a climate of healing in a violent society. *Young Children, 52*(7), 68–70.

Learners being teased, taunted, and bullied can take serious emotional and psychological tolls. Methods and Strategies 1.7 looks at ways to avoid students experiencing psychological violence.

Methods and Strategies 1.7: Stopping Teasing, Taunting, and Bullying

1. Work to stop all teasing, taunting, and bullying, both in the classroom and playground—no one should feel psychologically abused at school.
2. Avoid students "making fun" of others due to disabilities and special needs placements.
3. Teach the dangers of sexual harassment and report all incidents to school authorities.
4. Work to stop negative statements and actions toward anyone because of his or her cultural or gender backgrounds.
5. Teach students that differences of opinion can be settled without name calling and hurtful comments.

The School as a Risk Factor

Some educators, especially those who conscientiously work to help learners at-risk, might not understand how school practices and policies can actually contribute to learners being placed at-risk. Still, some educational practices, e.g., grouping learners by ability, expecting learners to sit for long periods of time, or providing work either too difficult or too easy may either cause or contribute to learners being placed at-risk. Schools can be stressful, boring, dangerous, and, generally speaking, harmful to students' overall progress. Students report that teachers do not understand them; they fear for their physical safety; they cannot complete homework assignments; and they do not or cannot participate in co-curricular or social activities (Crist, 1991).

Other conditions indicating the school might contribute to learners being at-risk include the current national obsession with testing and assessment, school violence, ability grouping, sexual harassment, and the emphasis on competition which separates learners into winners and losers.

Methods and Strategies 1.8 suggests ways educators can reduce schools' negative effects.

Methods and Strategies 1.8:
Reducing Schools' Negative Effects

Educators can reduce schools' negative effects on learners by:

1. Acknowledging when educational practices (such as ability grouping, threat of grade retention, and too many classroom rules) might place learners at-risk.

2. Determining appropriate and inappropriate practices that might contribute to the success of one student and to the failure of another.

3. Avoiding competitive activities and encouraging cooperative activities.

4. Understanding *individual* students, how they learn, their goals and frustrations, and educational practices that contribute to their academic and overall success.

Summary

Educating learners at-risk requires educators to understand at-risk conditions and behaviors as well as know how to identify specific elementary and middle school students at-risk. Identification tasks are not easy—a learner who is at-risk this semester might not be next semester. Or one learner might be at-risk and another might not, yet they share similar conditions and behaviors. Such tasks also require educators to develop a mindset that all learners might sometimes be at-risk. In fact, average learners can experience at-risk conditions and behaviors. Elementary and middle school educators who commit to help learners at-risk meet their professional responsibilities and also help learners at-risk.

Additional Information and Resources

Magera, D., & Wood, G. (1999). *Partnerships for at-risk learners.* These authors propose that one-quarter of American learners at-risk can be best addressed with a coordinated network of program options offering a variety of perspectives and methods. http://www.educ.wsu.edu/vision/coe05.html

Santa, C. M., & Hoien, T. (1999). An assessment of Early Steps: A program for early intervention of reading problems. *Reading Research Quarterly, 34*(1), 54–79. These authors compared the Early Steps and Reading Recovery reading programs and concluded that Early Steps makes a significant difference as an early intervention to reading problems.

U.S. Department of Education. (1999). *National Institute of the Education of At-Risk Students.* This institute provides a wealth of information on learners at-risk and appropriate educational experiences. http://www.ed.gov/offices/OERI/At-Risk/

Chapter 2	# Characteristics of Effective At-Risk Programs

Overview

What are the characteristics of effective at-risk programs, those essentials that make a difference in the lives of children from kindergarten through the eighth grade? What should K–8 educators include in programs that actually achieve positive results? Why should designers and implementors of programs for learners at-risk focus on more than one at-risk condition or behavior rather than placing emphasis only on the factor causing the learner to be at-risk? These and other questions are addressed in this chapter on characteristics of effective at-risk programs.

Chapter Objectives

After reading and thinking about this chapter on characteristics of effective at-risk programs, the reader should be able to:

1. Explain several reasons why programs for learners at-risk need to address more than one condition or behavior.
2. Explain why programs should comprehensively address self-esteem, have high expectations, teach social skills, provide for educators and students agreeing on educational expectations, involve parents, and focus on motivation and success.
3. Name examples of effective programs that address specific at-risk conditions or behaviors.
4. Suggest criteria for evaluating the extent to which programs and efforts address at-risk conditions and behaviors.
5. Offer several suggestions for designing and implementing at-risk programs that have the potential for making a difference in the lives of K–8 learners.
6. Offer a rationale for educators providing a sense of community and for demonstrating genuine concern for students at-risk.

7. Name additional sources of information for learning about other programs, the population at-risk, and the purposes of the programs.

Effective At-Risk Programs: Several Fundamental Beliefs

Research we have conducted, lessons we have learned from grants supporting programs for K–8 learners at-risk, and first-hand experiences with learners at-risk and their parents and educators have contributed to several fundamental beliefs. First, learners at-risk deserve the professional attention of caring, competent, and concerned educators and administrators. Second, a learner is rarely at-risk due to just one factor or condition, and therefore, effective programs need to address more than one condition or behavior. Third, students' at-risk conditions and behaviors can be identified and assessed. Fourth, learners at-risk can be provided effective programs and efforts designed to improve academic achievement and social skills, as well as reduce at-risk behaviors and conditions. Fifth, learners at-risk deserve equal access to high-quality educational programs that reflect collaborative and coordinated efforts to address academic and social needs. Sixth, effective programs can be replicated as well as designed and implemented.

Characteristics of Effective At-Risk Programs

As with all educational efforts, some at-risk programs work better than others. After considering individual K–8 learners and their respective at-risk factors, educators can identify characteristics of programs that address specific needs. Then, a program can either be adopted or can be designed and implemented. Regardless of the choice, successful at-risk programs seem to have eight essential characteristics that contribute to their effectiveness.

Characteristic 1—Provides comprehensive programs and efforts.

Addressing more than just a single at-risk condition or an isolated problem greatly enhances the success of programs for learners at-risk. Few, if any, at-risk conditions result from a single factor. For example, efforts to convince a sexually active eighth grader of the dangers of pregnancy or sexually transmitted diseases will be more successful if efforts also focus on improving self-esteem, demonstrating the importance of attending school on a regular basis, showing how school success affects one's future, and giving extra help to youngsters living in urban areas and in poverty.

Case Study 2.1 tells about Project Enable, an at-risk program addressing multiple conditions and behaviors.

 ## Case Study 2.1: Project Enable

A large university and a local school system formed a collaborative effort called Project Enable, a program designed for middle school learners at-risk.

Project Enable consisted of a collaborative partnership of university faculty, teachers and administrators, preservice teacher education students, parents, and community representatives. The preservice teachers provided individualized instruction, advisory experiences, and positive role models for learners at-risk. Four overall goals included: 1) curricular materials should address both academic and behavioral needs of learners at-risk; 2) educational experiences, both in-class and community experiences, should teach learners at-risk about career possibilities and educational opportunities; 3) advisement efforts and activities should improve self-esteem; and 4) educational and advisory experiences should include appropriate behavior, interpersonal skills, and methods of dealing with conflict and anger.

The educators provided materials such as computer software and high-interest books, especially designed for middle school learners at-risk. Curricular materials and software fostered higher levels of thinking and allowed students increased enjoyment in learning, especially software replicating real-life situations. These materials addressed students' diverse learning styles and wide range of academic achievement. Also, teachers provided personal organizational materials (e.g., planners and organizational notebooks) to help students learn effective work habits and to plan effective use of time.

The middle school students participated in 1) community trips to places that would make them more aware of technology and possible careers in technology fields; 2) advisement efforts and activities designed to improve self-esteem—educators provided opportunities to promote students' self-esteem such as being given the opportunity (and the accompanying responsibilities) to leave the traditional classroom; 3) educational experiences that taught them life options and possibilities, i.e., materials and experiences that showed the connection between staying in school (and demonstrating acceptable behavior and working toward academic achievement) and being able to have life options and possibilities; and 4) educational experiences and advisement efforts to teach appropriate behavior, interpersonal skills, and methods of dealing with conflict.

Also, parents and families served on advisory boards and, whenever possible, in actual learning experiences—a main premise of Project Enable focused on involving parents, both in planning and implementing the overall program.

Characteristic 2—Recognizes that self-esteem affects achievement.

The powerful impact of learners' self-esteem on their academic achievement and social well-being has enormous implications for addressing the needs of populations at-risk. An individual's self-esteem continually accumulates experiences that "tell" the individual his or her degree of self-worth. The self-esteem consists of everyday happenings, good and bad, that the learner experiences. Unfortunately, school and home experiences, both of which should contribute positively to the self-esteem do just the opposite.

The implications of self-esteem development for learners at-risk or potentially at-risk should never be underestimated. Too many negative experiences can destroy the learner's belief in him- or herself. Parents damage self-esteem and make at-risk conditions more acute when they constantly tell a child what his or her abilities do not allow, discourage new pursuits to avoid possible failure, and set unrealistic goals. The school can be an equal culprit when it groups learners by ability so that slow learners stay together all day and when school officials reprimand students for their lack of academic abilities. The learner at-risk, whether at-risk due to reading abilities or low socioeconomic status, may become "less at-risk" when educators address the self-esteem. Teachers know that learners feel better about themselves when they do better in school, and vice-versa (Canfield, 1990).

Methods and Strategies 2.1 examines Jack Canfield's ten-step method to strengthen students' self-esteem.

Methods and Strategies 2.1: Improving Self-Esteem

The Canfield program uses a ten-step method to help strengthen students' self-esteem and to increase their chances for success in life. This program proposes that educators can improve children's self-esteem on a daily basis by encouraging them to have positive attitudes and self-perceptions. Canfield's ten-step program includes 1) teachers accepting responsibility for the learner's self-esteem; 2) focusing on the positive; 3) teachers' monitoring their comments; 4) using student support groups in the classroom; 5) identifying strengths and resources; 6) clarifying visions so motivation can result; 7) setting goals and objectives; 8) using visualization to release creativity and alter perceptions of the environment; 9) taking appropriate action; and 10) responding appropriately to feedback (Canfield, 1990).

Characteristic 3—Teaches social skills needed for successful interaction.

Many learners at-risk, like many other learners, simply do not have the social skills necessary for positive social interaction. The problems of learners at-risk can grow more acute due to their inability to interact socially, to understand the necessity of working cooperatively toward goals, and to realize the need for positive conflict resolution. Effective at-risk programs provide deliberate and planned activities to address this lack of social skills.

In one of our experiences with learners at-risk, one young boy who lacked social skills did not like to work with cooperative groups. On one occasion, he stated, "I can do it better alone." In fact, in most cases, he probably could work better alone; however, his teacher wanted him to work cooperatively with others. This conscientious teacher made a deliberate effort to teach the young boy how to work with others—how to communicate, deal with differing opinions, and how to work toward shared goals. Eventually, his attitudes toward the group changed. Admittedly, he probably would have still preferred to work alone, but at least he had learned the social skills needed for positive group interaction.

Methods and Strategies 2.2 looks at several aspects for evaluating whether a program or effort teaches social skills.

 ## Methods and Strategies 2.2: Social Skills

Teaching social skills and positive social interaction should include:

1. Teaching students how to interact socially during the school day—all forms of peer involvement, group work, social situations, school parties, hall interactions, field trips, and all situations requiring social interactions during the school day.
2. Teaching communications skills—how to listen effectively, speak forcefully yet politely, disagree in a constructive manner, and portray positive body language.
3. Teaching conflict resolution and how to resolve interpersonal problems in a positive, healthy manner.
4. Teaching how to work and engage in cooperative learning, peer tutoring, and other collaborative projects where students share common goals and accept responsibility for specific tasks.
5. Teaching students to work with learners from other cultures, gender, and social classes, realizing that learning partners and friends can come from people different from themselves.
6. Teaching students to engage in productive behaviors with adults (e.g., educators, administrators, and parents) who want to help them and support their learning efforts.
7. Teaching learners to role play specific situations such as dealing with frustration, refusing to succumb to peer pressure, responding to conflict, and avoiding unnecessary confrontations as well as responding positively when confrontations are unavoidable.

The New Haven School-Community Connection provides an excellent example of an at-risk program that includes a special social skills curriculum. Called *A Social Skills Curriculum for Inner-City Children*, James Comer's program permits low-income, disproportionately high-risk children to gain some of the same skills that children from better-educated and higher-income families often gain simply by participating in the activities of their families. Problem solving rather than fault finding becomes a major focus of the program. To accomplish this goal, Comer's program integrates the teaching of basic academic skills, social skills, and artistic expression and includes all the skills needed for successful social interaction.

Characteristic 4—Provides opportunities for agreement on goals, methods, and materials.

The increased knowledge of development in K–8 students has provided a sound basis for developmentally appropriate educational experiences. Learners at-risk and their educators, however, need to agree on expectations, methods, and materials. Perceptive educators realize that learners at-risk might perceive expectations differently, might benefit from alternative methods, and might demonstrate greater achievement with certain kinds of materials. Rather than imposing additional obstacles to the success of learners at-risk, educators and learners at-risk can collaborate on expectations and educational experiences. Not only do learners at-risk have a more tailored program, but they also perceive educators as genuinely wanting to assist with their academic and social progress.

The DeLaSalle Education Center in Kansas City provides opportunities for teachers and students to agree on learning materials, methods, and expected results. This program accepts largely inner-city African American males who have educational and behavioral deficiencies. After agreeing with the students on materials, methods, and expected results, teachers modify their teaching styles to match learners' preferred learning styles. The DeLaSalle program provides students with a team of teachers who are responsible for making major educational decisions, counselors, administrators, psychoeducational assessment specialists, and a "Safe Teacher," who pledges unconditional positive regard for the student.

Another teacher team who works with students at-risk, both academically and behaviorally, meets with each student at the beginning of the year to determine the extent of her or his conditions or behaviors, administers learning style inventories, discusses testing with her or him (i.e., on what kinds of tests they do best, how they feel during tests, and how they study for tests), asks about personal goals for learning and behavior, and helps her or him set both short-term and long-term goals. Teachers and students revisit these goals every six weeks and determine whether progress has been made. Sometimes, during these conferences, students change goals (sometimes with the encouragement of the teacher), but teachers and students always know and agree on the goals as well as the methods and materials the student will use to reach the goals.

Methods and Strategies 2.3 provides an example of a Learning Agreement form. Teachers can use the form as a beginning point and make revisions to meet individual needs.

Methods and Strategies 2.3:
Preparing a Learning Agreement

Learning Agreement

Date _____

Student _____

Teacher _____

Period beginning and ending dates _____

Subject(s) _____

Learning Goals

1. _____

2. _____

3. _____

Behavior Goals

1. _____

2. _____

3. _____

Learning Methods/Strategies/Learning Style/Assessment

_____

_____

_____

Materials

_____

_____

Student Signature_____ Teacher Signature _____

Characteristic 5—Places priority on high expectations.

Programs for gifted and talented learners place learners in intellectually stimulating situations and expect learners to meet high proficiency levels; at-risk programs, however, often fail to demand excellence from learners due to low expectations. Rather than allowing or even promoting mediocrity, at-risk programs should be challenging and rigorous and have high expectations. Students can achieve in such programs when educators provide appropriate objectives, methods, and materials.

The Accelerated Schools for Disadvantaged Students program educates academically learners at-risk by having high expectations, providing deadlines by which students are to be performing at grade level, offering stimulating instructional programs, having educational staff that offer the program do the planning, and using all available parental and community resources. These efforts should close the achievement gap after a period of intervention so that students can return to regular instruction. This approach also addresses serious achievement deficits—the single most important reason why students drop out of school. The accelerated curriculum seeks to bring all learners up to grade level rather than limiting interventions to "pull-out" programs. Two features contribute to the program's success and should be considered in developing other at-risk programs: the program involves parents, and it includes an extended school day that provides rest periods, arts activities, and time for independent assignments or homework (Hopfenberg, Lewin, Meister, & Rogers, 1991).

The LEAP (Learning and Education Acceleration Program) is a Winston-Salem, NC, school program that helps learners at-risk of academic achievement catch up with their peers by completing two years of academic course work in a single, 200-day academic year. The school philosophy is high expectations make for higher achievement; instead of making the curriculum easier, the LEAP school provides an accelerated course of study. The students are taught how to clear the hurdles—they must have a 90% attendance, must pass all classes, and must pass a competency test for the grade they wish to skip (Harrison, 1998).

Characteristic 6—Involves parents and families.

James Griffith (1998) suggested parents thought schools should encourage them to take a more active role in educating their children, especially since a link exists between parents' involvement and positive student outcomes. Despite the benefits of parent involvement, educators continue to be dissatisfied with parents' involvement in schools. Also, gaps often exist between parents' and teachers' expectations for parents involvement. Educators often interpret parents' lack of involvement as showing little concern for their children's education. In contrast, parents often perceive school staff as not wanting their participation (Griffith, 1998). We feel Griffith's concern might be even more acute for learners at-risk and their parents. Some parents might be hesitant to attend school functions due to embarrassment, lack of understanding of at-risk conditions and behaviors, and concern that educators might not want their participation. Even with these obstacles and challenges, we think parent involvement is crucial to effective programs for learners at-risk.

One survey of eighth graders and their parents revealed that two-thirds of the students never or rarely discussed classes or school programs with parents; one-quarter of the parents never or rarely checked homework; half of the parents had not attended a school meeting since the beginning of the year; two-thirds of the parents had never talked with school officials about the academic program; and only one-third of the parents belonged to the parent-teacher organization (1991). These findings indicate the need to reengage parents and families in the educational process, especially for learners at-risk. Partnerships between parents and school personnel enhance the education of learners and provide parents with opportunities to play crucial roles in young adolescents' health and safety, in preparing them for school, and in creating a home environment that contributes to school achievement and overall development.

Methods and Strategies 2.4 suggests ways to involve parents and families.

Methods and Strategies 2.4:
Involving Parents and Families

1. Provide parents with both written and oral information about at-risk conditions and behaviors and convince them they can play integral roles in helping their children.
2. Provide parents with information about ways they can help learners at-risk, both at home and at school.
3. Let students at-risk know that parental involvement is needed and wanted.
4. Plan projects (both at school and away from school) that include as many family members as possible.
5. Help all teachers and administrators realize the importance of parental involvement, thus making parent involvement a school-wide effort.
6. Recruit (and work to obtain the support of) community members who are interested in being involved in schools and in assisting students at-risk.
7. Help parents feel comfortable at school—many of them might have also experienced at-risk behaviors and conditions.
8. Recognize parents' scheduling problems and offer a number of scheduling plans.
9. Implement a parent telephone tree that informs parents of information on students, at-risk conditions and behaviors, and ways parents can help.
10. Videotape educational programs for parents who were unable to attend meetings.

We have found that parent education programs can be helpful, especially for parents who lack understanding of at-risk conditions and behaviors and who might not know how to help their children. Many teachers in the early childhood years have well-developed parent education programs; unfortunately, parent education programs have not been as popular in the upper elementary schools and middle schools. Although schools should develop parent education programs specifically for individual learners and their parents, programs have been developed that help parents with at-risk conditions and behaviors, promote family involvement in children's lives, teach parents techniques for changing behaviors, help parents change their own negative behaviors, and teach parents how to address their children's problems.

Parent education programs for parents of children at-risk are needed for several reasons: 1) understanding at-risk conditions and behaviors; 2) responding appropriately to children at-risk; and 3) understanding at-risk programs. The parent education program should be planned to address specific needs rather than having parents attend to learn about general conditions and behaviors that their child might not be experiencing. Topics that might be addressed include (but not limited to): types and severity of at-risk conditions and behaviors, school responsibilities, educators' roles in helping children, parents' responsibilities and roles, special school at-risk programs, and community and social service agencies. Any effective parent education effort should also include a question and answer session.

Barbara Come and Anthony Fredericks (1995) explained a literacy program at Pulaski Elementary School in Savannah, GA. Pulaski is an inner-city school where 95% of the children are minority and from low socioeconomic backgrounds. The school developed a family literacy program for learners at-risk—the program provided special help in language and literacy development while increasing parental involvement in children's education through reading books. The overall goal of the program was to develop high self-esteem in children at an early age through parental encouragement and support of literacy development. The specific objectives included 1) increase students' reading achievement; 2) improve students' and parents' attitudes toward reading; 3) increase parental involvement in the school; 4) increase the amount of quality time families spend together; 5) foster home-school connections; and 6) create lifelong readers who stay in school and become productive citizens who believe in their own self-worth.

Characteristic 7—Focuses on the link between motivation and success.
Some learners at-risk, for one reason or another, might not be sufficiently motivated to address the condition that contributes to their lack of success. Also, lack of motivation can be an at-risk condition in and of itself. Although educators need to plan motivational strategies, learners should be encouraged to accept responsibility for their achievement and behavior. Regardless of the

program or the condition being addressed, the effectiveness of programs will be determined by students' motivation to overcome the at-risk condition.

Although not an at-risk program per se, Alderman (1990) proposes a "Links to Success" model that is designed to help students learn to link success and failures to their own efforts. While many students persist and work on their own for intrinsic reasons, other students work because of teacher demands and do not see their actions as related to success and failure. Alderman's model can help educators to motivate low achieving students to achieve by showing the learner how he or she contributes to the successful venture. The "Links to Success" model recognizes links such as goals, learning strategies, successful experiences, and attributions for success. These links provide a framework for fostering self-responsibility for learning—goals all learners at-risk need to work toward.

Alderman's (1990) suggested model holds promise for K–8 educators who work daily to motivate students to learn. Students, especially those in the upper elementary or middle school grades, have various preoccupations that interfere with their motivation and overall academic achievement. Therefore, educators need to strive to show learners at-risk how motivation, persistence, and determination affect one's success.

Methods and Strategies 2.5 looks at how to motivate the unmotivated child, a problem found in many schools today.

 ## Methods and Strategies 2.5: RISE—Motivating the Unmotivated Child

Edward Hootstein (1998) described the RISE model of motivating unmotivated children.

Relevant subject matter

1) Relate content to students' needs, interests, and expectations.

Example: A first grade teacher senses boredom with her students during a booktalk about *The Gingerbread Man* and *The Three Little Pigs*, so she asks a question such as "Have you ever seen a stranger you did not trust?"

2) Communicate the intended value of the learning activity. The teacher can make statements such as "It's important that you know how . . . " or "It's valuable to read these poems because . . ."

Interesting instruction

1) Pique students' curiosity by providing thought-provoking information.

Example: The teacher may say, "There is a coast off of Florida where many ships have disappeared without a clue. Can you explain why?"

2) Promote learners' sense of control in the learning process.

    Example: Offer students a choice of what they learn, how, and when they learn.

Satisfied learner

Provide rewards that motivate and capture attention.

    Example: Offer students feedback to let them know how they are doing such as "You explained it clearly" or "Your story is imaginative."

Expectations of success

1) Emphasize that increased effort will likely lead to success.

    Example: Provide feedback that motivates as well as lets students know how they are doing such as "It is good to see your hard work help you do so well."

Characteristic 8—Provides a sense of community.

Eric Schaps and Catherine Lewis (1998) described a sense of community as "a student's experience of being a valued, influential, contributing participant in a group whose members are committed to each others's learning, growth, and welfare" (p. 24–25).

Effective at-risk programs provide a sense of community—a belief or feeling that supports mutual expectations and positive relations as well as provides models of behavior for students. The ways in which teachers and administrators relate to students teach students a great deal about how people should be treated. Several attributes of interpersonal relations in schools, especially ones associated with school effectiveness, include students feeling cared about and respected, teachers sharing a vision and sense of purpose, teachers and students maintaining free and open communication, and teachers and students sharing a deep sense of respect. Ten specific elements that characterize positive adult and student relations in school communities include: shared vision, shared sense of purpose, shared values, incorporation of diversity, communication, participation, caring, trust, teamwork, and respect and recognition. Schools that conscientiously work at strengthening these elements usually build the necessary foundation for excellence (Rossi & Springfield, 1995).

Paula Groves (1998) agreed that at-risk programs need to develop a culture of caring. In her discussion of the Day and Night School, an alternative education program for students at-risk, she maintained that successful programs did more than just teach. Effective programs provided a culture of caring or a sense of family among students, teachers, administrators, and staff. For the Day and Night School, the familial school culture kept many of the students in school. The school adopted a buddy system where all staff members are assigned six students with whom they maintain close contact. This sense of community instilled a sense of accountability and ownership for the school and students because all staff members felt responsible for the students. They also demonstrated this sense of caring by providing weekly assessments of student progress, talking to students about problems, making phone calls home to students who have missed classes, and providing referrals to support agencies (Groves, 1998).

Effective school communities for learners at-risk can include educational experiences that 1) teach people to feel a part of a caring culture; 2) model how people can improve; 3) build close interpersonal relationships; 4) teach and demonstrate peoples' roles in a democratic society; 5) explain the basic human need to be a part of a group; 6) teach the importance of trust and respect; and 7) create new and dynamic relationships. Progress can be made toward these goals when educators provide comprehensive guidance and counseling programs, opportunities for curricular and social exploration, positive school environments, cooperative planning among educators and learners, and organizational arrangements which promote a sense of community such as heterogeneous grouping, cooperative learning, peer tutoring, and peer mentoring.

Methods and Strategies 2.6 shows how educators can strive toward the goal of community.

Methods and Strategies 2.6:
Developing a Sense of Community

In the development of a spirit of community, K–8 educators and their students can:

- Choose a name, motto, or logo which can be displayed on a banner or tee shirt (an attempt to "define" the group).
- Create events to celebrate group unity such as celebrations of member or community achievements.
- Use unifying daily classrooms or school rituals.
- Collaborate on events such as field trips, parties, and cooperative adventures.
- Keep an ongoing record of community life such as a scrapbook or a photograph album.
- Build bonding experiences at least twice yearly such as a retreat, a campout, a family math night, or a school-wide carnival.
- Foster ownership of the community physical environment by involving members in exploring, organizing, and improving the school and classroom (Graves, 1992).

Also, curricular, organizational practices and behavior policies should reflect an appreciation of community and its contributions. Educators cannot teach and promote the concept of community yet continue to plan in isolation, ignore students' needs, and practice exclusivity. For example, the curriculum needs to reflect the benefits of shared concerns and working together (such as contributions of groups); organizational strategies that emphasize group approaches such as cooperative learning and peer helpers; and school policies such as students having a voice in school rules. Traditional school practices such as teaching competition and individualism at the expense of collaboration, homogeneous grouping practices promoting exclusivity, and school policies solely written from educators' perspectives will not promote caring cultures.

While James X. Bembry refers to middle schools in Research and Classroom Practice 2.1: Forming an Educative Community, his ideas apply to other grade levels as well.

 ## Research and Classroom Practice 2.1: Forming an Educative Community

James X. Bembry describes Project SUCCESS (Schools, Universities, Community, Committed to Excellence in Service and Scholastics) which provides a comprehensive community service program to Baltimore middle school students who are considered at-risk academically, socially, or economically.

The program has involved more than 1,500 students by providing them with intensive, weekly service to the elderly in nursing homes. The selected sixth grade students are invited to attend a recruitment and orientation session during which they learn the problems facing the elderly.

Students are asked to make a commitment of at least once a week for one to three years. Students are given release time from school, are paired with an elderly partner, and students visit for one-hour. Examples of projects include discussions to build relationships, collaboration on arts and crafts projects, constructing family trees, sensory stimulation exercises, and field trips. Students maintain a weekly journal and attend reflective sessions once a month. These sessions provide opportunities for students to discuss experiences, challenges, and successes. Another goal is to build social and academic skills such as critical thinking, communication, trust, problem solving, and self-esteem.

Source: Bembry, J. X. (1998). Forming an educative community in the village. *Middle School Journal 30*(1), 18–24.

At-Risk Programs: Categories of Components

While we feel the previously-mentioned eight characteristics have merit for designing and implementing effective at-risk programs, other writers (Finn, 1989; Weir, 1996) prefer to look at at-risk programs in terms of categories of components, i.e., organizational, instructional, and interpersonal. Instead of considering the characteristics and organizational components as an "either-or" situation, perceptive educators will see their complementary nature. In fact, many aspects listed under each component are actually similar to the characteristics discussed above. Table 2.1 shows the three categories of components and selected descriptors under each.

Table 2.1—Components of Effective At-Risk Programs

Organizational Components

- Low student-teacher ratio.
- Environments similar to traditional educational settings.
- Links to outside agencies and community organizations.
- Fair and equitable discipline policies.
- Student participation in decision-making processes.
- Program designs for specific at-risk conditions and behaviors.
- Staff development on effective communicational strategies.

Instructional Components

- Attendance improvement projects.
- Effort on teaching student goal-setting.
- Cooperative learning and peer tutoring.
- Computer-assisted instruction.
- Wide range of instructional techniques.
- Integrated curriculum and interdisciplinary projects.
- Wide variety of curricular materials.
- Accelerated learning to gain skills equivalent to peers.

Interpersonal Components

- Effective communication between all parties.
- Caring and sensitive teachers and staff who choose to work with students at-risk.
- Supportive climate tailored to individual needs and abilities.
- Development of students' self-esteem.
- Development of positive attitudes toward school.
- Increased interactions between students and teachers.
- Development of a sense of community.
- Parent and community participation.
- Counseling designed for students at-risk.

Adapted from: Finn (1990) and Weir (1996).

Suggestions for Designing and Implementing At-Risk Programs

Suggestions for designing and implementing at-risk programs and efforts include:

1. Providing an at-risk program that is developmentally appropriate, i.e., teachers do not use a program designed for kindergartners and first grade with middle schoolers (and vice-versa).
2. Addressing more than one at-risk condition or behavior.
3. Involving teachers, administrators, parents, and community organizations in collaborative efforts.
4. Teaching learners to accept responsibility for academic achievement, behaviors, and long-term educational plans.
5. Planning efforts that extend a number of years, so learners at-risk as well as educators can realize long-term results.
6. Providing efforts that address both academic and non-academic needs (e.g., increasing self-esteem and teaching useful ways to use leisure time).
7. Preparing learners at-risk for instructional and advisory experiences, so they will understand expectations and learning outcomes.
8. Ensuring all programs and experiences have "real-world" perspectives, so learners understand how instructional and advisement experiences relate to their life.
9. Providing learners at-risk with supplemental educational opportunities provided by mentors who serve as positive role models.
10. Ensuring students feel a sense of community or caring—they feel educators care about their overall welfare as well as their academic progress.

Summary

The likelihood of an at-risk program being effective can be increased when educators include key characteristics that have contributed to the success of other programs. Although the characteristics and program components mentioned in this chapter have the potential for increasing a program's success, emphasizing all the characteristics and components can have an even greater effect. Using these program characteristics and components, educators of students at-risk can either replicate programs or design and implement original programs. Another possibility might be to consider existing programs to determine "what works" and then design a program based on the needs of a specific student population. Regardless of whether educators replicate or design programs, understanding these characteristics and components and basing programs on the specific conditions and behaviors of K–8 learners can contribute significantly to the success of at-risk programs and, subsequently, to the lives of learners.

Additional Information and Resources

At-Risk Students. URL: www.naesp.org/ntwrknws.htm This Title 1 School-wide Project Network is a program co-sponsored by NAESP to benefit schools with students at-risk.

Gullatt, D. E., & Lofton, B. D. (1998). Helping at-risk learners succeed: A whole-school approach to success. *Schools in the Middle, 7*(4), 11–14, 42–43. These authors describes a whole-school approach to helping learners at-risk and specifically offeres information on Success For All, assessment, continuous progress, mentoring, and instructional technology.

Lange, C. M. (1998). Characteristics of alternative schools and programs serving at-risk students. *The High School Journal, 81*(4), 183–198. Although Lange discusses at-risk programs in high schools, her article still offers valuable information about types of and characteristics of effective programs.

The Toolroom: Resource: Programs for Students At-Risk, Elementary and Secondary Schools. URL: www.newhorizons.org/trm_atriskreform.html. The Toolroom provides names and descriptions of replicable programs for students placed at-risk in elementary and secondary schools.

Chapter 3	# Methods, Strategies, and Assessment

Overview

Educators of learners at-risk sometimes ask, "What methods, strategies, and assessment should I use with learners at-risk? "What should I consider when planning educational experiences for these learners?" "Should we really assess these students who are already at-risk?" In this chapter, we will look at these and other questions as we suggest essential considerations, explain the importance of addressing multiple intelligences and learning styles, and suggest selected instructional methods and strategies that can be used with learners at-risk.

Chapter Objectives

After reading and thinking about this chapter on methods, strategies, and assessment, the reader should be able to:

1. Explain the importance of planning and implementing instruction for *specific* at-risk conditions and behaviors.
2. Explain why educators need to address students' individual abilities, previous achievement, interests, and curricular relevance.
3. Explain the importance of planning for multiple intelligences to address students' areas of strengths and weaknesses.
4. Offer several reasons for providing educational experiences that reflect students' learning styles.
5. Suggest several instructional methods and strategies that are appropriate for learners at-risk.
6. Suggest several appropriate purposes for assessing learners at-risk.

Planning Appropriate Educational Experiences
Essential Considerations

At-Risk Conditions and Behaviors

Teachers need to identify specific conditions and behaviors that indicate or place students at-risk. Throughout this book, we maintain that educational experiences for learners at-risk need to be "individualized" as much as possible. Methods, strategies, and assessment need to be focused toward the *specific* at-risk condition or behavior. For example, a high-achieving student who is at-risk of drug use needs educational experiences different from a potential school dropout. Likewise, a student who is learning disabled needs different educational plans than one who needs his or her specific learning styles or multiple intelligences addressed. One low achiever might prefer to work competitively with a group of friends; another might prefer cooperative learning or some other collaborative effort.

Abilities and Previous Achievement

Programs for students at-risk, specific instructional plans, and the daily implementation of instruction should be based upon carefully-determined abilities and previous achievement. A student reading on a third grade level will learn little when teachers provide instruction on a seventh grade level (and vice-versa). Both low-ability and high-ability students need to be challenged, according to their ability levels. Planning and implementing educational experiences based on abilities and previous achievement makes sound educational sense—students should feel more capable and confident (and feel less frustration); should actually achieve more short-term and long-term academic successes; and should develop more positive attitudes toward school.

Learner Interest and Curricular Relevance

Depending on their at-risk behaviors or conditions, students at-risk might have experienced a loss of motivation or interest in school work. Maybe they felt frustrated learning "stuff they would never use" as one middle school student told us. "Why do we have to learn all this book crap that will never do us any good?" another one asked. Encouraging students by offering statements such as "You will need this when you get to high school." or "Wait until you get to college—this will really help you then!" will likely prove unproductive. Teachers need to determine student interest and, then, make the curriculum relevant to their perspectives. One school we know about took their middle school students to a special "Career Fair" that focused on areas of interest. Although the teachers carefully avoided directing students toward particular careers, they did explain how "what was being studied at their school" related to "future careers."

Siowck-Lee Gan (1999) suggested motivating students at-risk through computer-based cooperative learning activities. Advantages of computer-based cooperative learning activities including instructional experiences can be individualized, students learn cooperation and interpersonal skills, and the computers serve as motivating devices (Gan, 1999). (While we cannot provide a comprehensive examination of Gan's work, the reference is listed in Additional Information and Resources.)

Methods and Strategies 3.1 shows how teachers can develop an inventory to determine learner interests.

Methods and Strategies 3.1: *Determining Learner Interests*

Teachers should develop their own interest inventories based on their students' backgrounds and at-risk conditions and behaviors. Examples of questions include: What do you do when you get home from school? What do you like to do on the weekends? What hobbies do you have? Do you like to collect things such as baseball cards or stamps? What is your favorite television program? How do you spend your summer vacations? What do you like and dislike about school? What are some books you like? What kinds of movies do you like? What books or magazines do you have at home? What do you want to learn about? What do you want me to know about you?

Planning for These Three Considerations

It has been our experience that generic or "one-size-fits-all" programs rarely work. For example, we know one program for students at-risk that places students in groups of eight. We think even eight is too large. It is unlikely that eight students have characteristics (e.g., at-risk conditions and behaviors, abilities and previous achievement, and learner interest) sufficiently similar to warrant similar instructional experiences and assessment devices.

To plan for these three considerations, teachers can use case histories, aptitude tests, attitude assessments, achievement test reports, anecdotal records, diagnostic testing results, teacher observation, teacher referrals, parental information, student interest inventories, social service agency reports, and in some cases, Individualized Education Plans. Readers undoubtedly can think of other ways to determine these essential considerations. Once these considerations have been determined, educators can, then, plan accordingly. We do not mean to downplay the difficulty associated with planning. Planning for a wide array of behaviors, conditions, abilities, achievement levels, and interests requires both commitment and expertise. Also, as we have previously stated, it will require individualization or at least small groups (i.e., groups of two or three) to some extent because of students' differences.

Multiple Intelligences

Howard Gardner (1993) believed learners have at least seven intelligences:

1. Logical mathematical—enjoy solving problems, finding patterns, outlining, calculating.
2. Linguistic—relate to the meaning of words, their rhythms and sounds.
3. Spatial—like to design, invent, imagine, and create.
4. Bodily kinesthetic—learn through physical movement, mimicking, and touching.
5. Musical/rhythmic—enjoy the human voice, environmental and instructional sounds.
6. Interpersonal—can understand the feelings of others.
7. Intrapersonal—understand own emotion, motivations, and moods.

Appropriateness for Learners At-Risk

Gardner's theory of multiple intelligences can help teachers engage learners at-risk in learning experiences, promote the development of specific intelligences that should be viewed as strengths, and address particular intelligences that students lack but are needed for school success. Addressing multiple intelligences requires educators to allow students to achieve at their own pace, assure students receive positive reinforcement, and help students reach their fullest potential, regardless of the intelligence. While teachers might say, "Addressing multiple intelligences is fine, but what about the overall curricular scope and sequence? There are so many things students need to learn." We agree—educators cannot be expected to allow students to "learn" only in their primary intelligences. We are suggesting, however, that teachers allow students to learn, whenever possible, in their primary areas of intelligence. Also, students should be encouraged to build upon special areas of intelligence as well as develop some of the lesser intelligences, especially those needed for success in the world outside the school (i.e., interpersonal skills).

Planning for Multiple Intelligences

After a careful and objective determination of students' multiple intelligences, teachers can begin to design instructional experiences that reflect students' strengths and weaknesses.

Judith Reiff (1997) provided an example of Civil War activities, based on multiple intelligences. Research and Classroom Practice 3.1: Planning for Multiple Intelligences provides a beginning point on how Civil War activities can reflect multiple intelligences.

Research and Classroom Practice 3-1:
Planning for Multiple Intelligences
Civil War—5th Grade
Margaret Tontillo

Linguistic.

The students pretend that they are Civil War soldiers living during that time period. They write letters back home to relatives or friends and describe events and their feelings. Include specific details which the students have learned about the Civil War. You can later dye the letters with tea to make them look more authentic! The students' letters would be used as a form of assessment.

Spatial

The students pretend that they are Union or Confederate soldiers during the Civil War. Have the students design maps which show their strategies, movements, and locations. The maps can be colorful and the students can later use them during role playing as props. The teacher can assess the students using their maps.

Interpersonal

As small groups, the students write plays about specific events which occurred during the Civil War. The students should work together and later evaluate their group members on participation and effort. Examples of major events include Lincoln's "Gettysburg Address" or a major battle. The play's content as well as participation in the group can be used for assessment purposes.

Intrapersonal

The students create Civil War board games independently. The games should include directions, game pieces, and the actual board. The students color their boards and have them laminated after the students are finished! The teacher can assess the students using the final products—the games!

Kinesthetic

The students act out important events which occurred during the Civil War. They use props and move around the room during their scenes, if appropriate. They can portray soldiers and march!

Musical

The students listen to music which was either written or popular in the 1860s. Discuss how the music has changed over the years. Afterwards, the students can write their own inspirational songs about America. The teacher can use the students' songs in order to assess the students' knowledge.

———————

Source: Reiff, J. (1997). Multiple intelligences, culture, and equitable learning. *Childhood Education, 73*(5), 301–304.

Judith Reiff (1996) also maintains that rather than promoting learning through students' strengths, schools sometimes develop elaborate systems for identifying weaknesses and labeling students at-risk according to prescribed deficiencies. This is all-too-often the case with learners at-risk at both the elementary and middle levels.

We often encourage teachers to direct more attention to what "students do right and less attention to what students do wrong." In doing so, we keep our feet firmly planted on the ground—we are sufficiently realistic to realize this is not always possible or even feasible. However, we continue to believe learners at-risk demonstrate more appropriate behavior, more academic achievement, and enjoy school more when their teachers view special intelligences as strengths on which to build educational experiences.

Learning Styles

While definitions of learning styles differ, we prefer the following: Learning styles are cognitive, affective, and physiological behaviors that indicate how learners perceive, interact with, and respond to educational experiences. These patterns of cognitive, affective, and physiological behavior indicate how individuals process information and respond to the affective, sensory, and environmental dimensions of the instruction process. It is important for educators to recognize that students have unique learning styles and to determine appropriate instructional methods and strategies that reflect students' styles of learning. Educators who understand learning styles and provide appropriate instruction can improve student achievement and behavior, increase student interest and enthusiasm toward school work, and gain student approval of instructional methods.

Marie Carbo and Helene Hodges (1988) suggest that many students at-risk have not been taught using instructional methods that meet their learning style preferences. The majority of learners at-risk learn best in an informal, highly structured environment. Learners at-risk tend to be significantly less visual and auditory and have higher preferences for tactile/kinesthetic stimuli and greater needs for mobility. They tend to be unmotivated or strongly adult-motivated, can concentrate and learn best with an adult or with peers, and are most alert during the morning hours. Many are global learners and, therefore, they learn best when teachers present information as a whole, consider the "whole" rather than specific parts, and are unconcerned with names, dates, and other specifics (Carbo & Hodges, 1988).

Appropriateness for Learners At-Risk

Research (Reiff, 1996) suggests that equating learning styles with teaching and learning activities contributes to meeting each individual's unique needs. There is not a right or wrong way to learn, but certain styles are more appropriate for certain situations. Styles do not always conform to standard approaches and often earn students labels such as "at-risk." The key is to determine learning styles and, then, provide educational experiences that address the styles. As Methods and Strategies 3.2 shows, educators can determine students' learning styles in several ways.

Methods and Strategies 3.2:
Using Learning Styles Inventories

Several learning styles inventories include:

1. Learning Style Inventory (LSI) (Dunn, Dunn, & Price, 1986) and the LSP Learning Style Profile (LSP) (Keefe & Monk, 1986). The Learning Style Inventory looks at many affective and physiological dimensions of learning styles such as environmental conditions, emotional needs, sociological needs, and physical needs.

2. NASSP Learning Style Profile (LSP) (Keefe & Monk, 1986), designed for older students, is also appropriate for grades 6–8 and looks at cognitive styles, perceptual responses, study and instructional preferences (Keefe & Monk, 1986).

3. Reading Style Inventory (RSI) provides specific information about children's strengths and preferences while reading and suggests appropriate teaching methods and strategies (Carbo & Hodges, 1988).

Planning for Learning Styles

Planning methods and strategies that reflect students' learning styles include using all types of questions (including factual questions and value questions); using advance organizers in an attempt to relate past and present learning experiences; setting clear purposes for learning experiences; using multisensory experiences, i.e., students listening as well as reading and speaking; and using a variety of review and reflection strategies (Cornett, 1983). Table 3.1 looks at several strategies for basing instruction on learning styles.

Providing educational experiences that address learning styles holds significant potential for contributing to success rather than leading to frustration. A problem for years has been that teachers assumed students all learn alike or in a manner (or style) similar to the teacher. An alternative is to consider how the students learn most effectively. For example, a teacher instructs a class on the Vietnam War, its beginnings, battles, and the U.S.'s eventual pull-out. The teacher lectures, shows slides, and perhaps allows students to work in groups. In other words, the teacher teaches in the way he or she learns most effectively. While the students are undoubtedly diverse, the teacher expects all learners, both girls and boys, to learn in the same manner or, in this case, to use the same styles. Some students studying an event such as the Vietnam War might want an "overall picture" and then focus on the details; other students learn better when they learn the specific events and then cognitively combine these events into a whole (Manning & Baruth, 1995).

Table 3.1—Strategies for Basing Instruction on Learning Styles

Several instructional strategies include:

1. *De-emphasize skill work requiring a strongly analytic learning style.*

2. *Begin all instruction globally and slowly proceed toward the details.*

3. *Involve the tactile and kinesthetic modalities of the learner and include many visuals.*

4. *Provide a structured and highly organized learning environment.*

5. *Allow students to work with peers, with another teacher, or alone, depending on their individual perspective.*

6. *Provide learners with special work areas, i.e., one that is quiet and one where students can talk.*

7. *Experiment with scheduling the most difficult subjects during the late morning and early afternoon hours.*

Developed from: Carbo, M., & Hodges, H. (1988). Learning styles strategies can help students at risk. Exceptional Children, 20(4), 55–58.

Case Study 3.1 looks at how the teaching team at Smith-Cranston Elementary School collaborated on teaching methods and strategies.

Case Study 3.1: The Teaching Team Collaborates on Selecting Methods and Strategies

The teaching team at Smith-Cranston Elementary School met periodically to discuss the proper educational experiences for the 32 learners at-risk for whom they were responsible. Each of the 4 members on the team worked with 8 students—each had a part-time paraprofessional who worked with them during the planning of instruction as well as the actual implementation. At a mid-semester meeting attended by one parent, the assistant principal, and two university professors, they revisited the issue of how best to meet the students' needs. Some teachers felt that what they had been doing was not working and wanted to ask others for input on the most effective instructional methods.

"Emily, how do you do it? You seem to be so successful with your students. What method do you use? You have good rapport, and your students make a lot of progress each year," asked Peter.

Emily responded, "I do not think I do anything too extraordinary. I just consider each student as an individual—then, Marge, the para-professional, and I do our best." Emily went on to explain that they did not use a *particular* method. They tried to consider each student, and then, employed a method that they thought would work with him or her. "We use cooperative learning with Bob, Janice, and Brennan. Alisha and Robin have almost completely individualized instruction. The other three work at learning centers. But they might not be doing this next week. We will consider their motivation, ability, and the material to be learned, and then decide the best method for them to learn," she said.

Emily and Marge explained that all their students had homework but not necessarily the same amount—some have less than others, but regardless of how little or much they have, they are held accountable. Homework is checked and all students are expected to do their best. Marge offered, "We also try to determine their primary intelligences and their preferred learning styles. Then, we build upon individual strengths and encourage students to learn in the style they prefer. We cannot say we have *a* method."

The discussion continued, but the major point kept returning to *individualized* consideration and attention. The group could not identify a particular method or a method that was designed specifically for learners at-risk. By the end of the meeting, Emily and Marge had about convinced the group to consider different methods for different learners. Instead of expecting all students to work at learning centers or all students to engage in cooperative learning, learners were considered as individuals—expectations, methods, and materials differed according a learners' ability, motivation, special intelligence, and specific at-risk condition or behavior.

Providing Appropriate Instructional Methods and Strategies

We think most learners at-risk benefit from methods and strategies designed for learners in general. However, these methods and strategies probably need to be modified to meet the special needs of learners at-risk. In one class we often visit, the teachers basically use methods (e.g., cooperative learning, demonstrations, learning centers, peer-tutoring, and projects) that are similar to those used by other teachers. However, carefully-planned accommodations reflect the needs of individualized learners. This section examines a number of methods and strategies that we think can be modified for learners at-risk.

Cooperative Learning

Learners at-risk often work better in collaborative groups where teachers encourage students to help one another. Many students, especially learners at-risk, do not respond well to competition. Competing for grades and for the teacher's time *might* work well for the "winners" and those who like to compete, but the "losers" or those who elect not to compete often feel like they are inadequate in some way.

Cooperative learning can be defined as an alternative instructional system in which students work in heterogeneous groups of four to six members and earn recognition, rewards, and sometimes grades based on the academic performance of their groups (Slavin, 1983). Cooperative learning can be an ideal means of capitalizing on students' desire to socialize with peers within a safe structure (Slavin, 1996). Plus, cooperative learning addresses the problems of learners at-risk experience such as lower self-esteem, lower academic achievement, and less-than-desirable social skills.

All cooperative learning methods share the idea that students work together to learn and are responsible for one another's learning as well as their own. In cooperative work, methods emphasize the use of team goals and team success which can only be achieved if all members of the team learn the objectives being taught. That is, students' tasks are not to do something as a team but to learn something as a team.

Three central concepts of effective cooperative learning include:

1. Team rewards—In these techniques, teams may earn certificates or other team rewards if they achieve above a designated criterion. Grades are not given based on team performance, but students may sometimes qualify for as many as 5 bonus points (on a 100 point scale) if their teams meet a high criterion of excellence. The teams are not in competition to earn rewards; all (or none) of the teams may achieve the criterion in a given week.

2. Individual accountability—This means that the team's success depends on the individual learning of all team members. This encourages team members to tutor one another and to make sure that everyone on the team is ready for a quiz or other assessment.

3. Equal opportunities for success—Students contribute to their teams by improving over their own past performance. This ensures that high, average, and low achievers are equally challenged to do their best, and the contributions of all team members will be valued.

Research on cooperative learning methods has indicated that team rewards and individual accountability are essential elements for producing basic skills achievement (Slavin, 1995). It is not enough to simply tell students to work together. They must have a reason to take one another's achievement seriously. Further, research indicates that if students are rewarded for doing better than they have in the past, they will be more motivated to achieve than if they are rewarded based on their performance in comparison to others, because rewards for improvement make success neither too difficult nor too easy for students to achieve (Slavin, 1996). Methods and Strategies 3.3 looks at how teachers might make cooperative learning decisions with their students.

Methods and Strategies 3.3:
Making Decisions About Cooperative Learning

Discuss with students (probably in groups of four) how a topic or concept might be learned through cooperative learning. Ask the students 1) what topic do *they* feel is most appropriate; 2) how they might divide learning responsibilities (i.e., the "roles" of each in the cooperative arrangement); 3) how they want to be assessed; and 4) how they can most appropriately present a summary or report to the class. Last, ask them what other considerations *they* think should be considered as they prepare for cooperative learning.

Demonstrations

Learners at-risk like demonstrations because of the active engagement in a learning activity rather than listening to the teacher. Less motivated or less capable readers also often like demonstrations. Demonstrations can be used to teach almost any subject and for a variety of purposes. The social studies teacher can demonstrate by role-playing or simulating. The mathematics teacher demonstrates the steps in solving a problem. The language arts teacher demonstrates clustering to students as a preparation for a writing assignment. Demonstrations serve a number of purposes: to assist in recognizing a solution to an existing problem, to bring closure to a lesson or unit of study, to demonstrate a thinking skill, to give students an opportunity for vicarious participation in active learning, to illustrate a particular point of content, to introduce a lesson or unit of study in an attention-getting manner, and to review. Teachers conducting demonstrations should decide the most effective way to conduct the demonstration (such as by the teacher, by another student, to the entire class, or to a small group); the most visible means whereby all students can observe; practice with the materials and procedures prior to demonstrating to the class; and appropriate pacing of the demonstration (Kellough & Kellough, 1999).

In our observations of learners at-risk, we have found that the most effective teachers carefully plan the demonstration. The reason for the demonstration also should be clear—while they are excellent attention-grabbers, they should be the most effective means of presenting information. In essence, demonstrations should not be conducted just for the sake of a demonstration. Also, careful thought should be given to whether students understand the concepts rather than just observing the demonstration itself. Table 3.2 provides several guidelines for using demonstrations with learners at-risk.

Table 3.2—Guidelines for Using Demonstrations

Teachers of learners at-risk should:

1. *Design the demonstration especially for learners at-risk, i.e., plan for lower attention spans, lower levels of motivation, or problems with higher-order thinking skills.*

2. *Explain the purpose or the objective of the demonstration in such a way learners realize how it relates to their lives.*

3. *Arrange the classroom, so all students can see and hear.*

4. *Develop sufficient confidence with the demonstration, so it can be confidently and effectively given.*

5. *Include only the necessary materials and equipment on the demonstration table to avoid distraction and confusion of learners at-risk.*

6. *"Close" the demonstration in such a way students will know the purpose as well as the outcome—perhaps ask the students such questions as: "Can you tell us the purpose of the demonstration, Emily?" "What was one part of the demonstration you particularly liked, Jan?"*

Drill and practice

Drill and practice must be carefully used with learners at-risk. As one teacher told us, "Drill and practice is one reason the students are at-risk. Teachers have turned them off with the boredom of drill." While we agree with this teacher to some extent, we also feel drill and practice has its use with learners at-risk, especially when correctly implemented. Table 3.3 provides several questions for teachers to ask prior to using drill and practice.

Table 3.3—Questions About Drill and Practice

- *Is it more than just "busy work?"*
- *Does it address a specific purpose?*
- *Is it carefully planned?*
- *Is it the most effective method to teach learners at-risk?*
- *Is it of sufficient length to hold learners' attention?*
- *Is it appropriate for the specific at-risk condition or behavior?*
- *Are students allowed to work collaboratively rather than competitively?*

The teacher answering affirmatively to the questions in Table 3.3 *will not* use drill and practice to keep students busy, will not rely on endless worksheets and workbooks, and will not allow satiation (i.e., when students have their "fill" of a particular topic of activity) to occur. The teacher will know if drill and practice is the most effective method of either teaching or reinforcing the specific curricular content. Again, we agree somewhat with the teacher who told us drill and practice contributes to some students being at-risk; but we still believe this method can be effective, especially when it is designed correctly and meets the needs of learners at-risk.

Exploratory Activities

As an instructional method, we see "exploratory activities" as opportunities for learners at-risk to explore *within the curricular areas*—not for a month, six weeks, or a semester, but for a more flexible length of time. Regardless of the curricular area, the student who develops a particular interest and has a desire to learn more should be given the opportunity. The learner who sees how a particular area of science or social studies can contribute to his or her individual life should be encouraged to "explore" the interest; the student in the language arts class who wants to learn to speak effectively in front of others should be given the opportunity to expand his or her abilities through exploration. We feel that exploratory activities are particularly important for learners at-risk. Teachers should always look for areas that learners consider relevant to their lives—those areas that relate to particular interests, regardless of whether the interests are ones the teacher would have recommended for exploration. These areas might be the motivating factor that "turns students on to learning" or motivates them to stay in school. Upon determination of exploratory areas, teachers then need to decide whether to let students work in small groups or independently. Teachers should also encourage students to decide how they can best explore the area, i.e., through reading, experimenting, inquiry approaches, or field trips. Some learners at-risk will give up a topic of exploration after only a short time; others might be so fascinated with the exploratory activity that it captures their attention for a longer time, perhaps well into the adult years.

Field Trips

Field trips can be a rich source of learning and exploration for both teachers and students. Unfortunately, school district rules, financial resources, and teachers' reluctance to take students on field trips often result in fewer trips. While we recognize the problems associated with field trips, we think learners at-risk should have the opportunity to leave the school. Field trips, when effectively planned and implemented, can have many advantages. First, they provide an opportunity for students to socialize outside the regular school setting. Second, learners can see the outside world (i.e., educational opportunities and career possibilities) as well as learn how to behave. Field trips, however, should not be a one-day lesson—they should relate to topics being studied in school and to the students' lives in some way. Teachers should carefully avoid students feeling "we have the day off." Instead, as table 3.4 explains, teachers should carefully explain the learning objectives of the field trip.

Table 3.4—Suggestions for Effective Field Trips

1. Clarify behavior expectations upfront, a day or two prior to the trip; instead of having 10 to 12 rules, have 3 or 4 broad rules (and the reasons for the rules) that learners can understand.

2. Clarify the learning objectives (both cognitive and affective) of the trip, so students will know the educational purposes of the trip.

3. Plan for student safety—think ahead to all possible problems and dangers and plan accordingly.

4. Make a preliminary trip to the location to determine its suitability for learners as well as its feasibility to meet the objectives of the learning experience.

5. Give students sufficient time to make the visit worthwhile and to meet the learning objectives of the trip.

6. Make the field trip as "interdisciplinary" as possible by helping students to see how the various curricula areas are reflected.

7. Conduct follow-up discussions of the trip to determine whether objectives were met and to provide students with opportunities to share their thoughts and opinions.

Educators sometimes wonder how to determine the most appropriate field trips for learners at-risk. Methods and Strategies 3.4 suggests way to determine appropriate field trips.

Methods and Strategies 3.4: Determining Appropriate Field Trips

Make an effort to determine the most appropriate field trips for learners at-risk. First, consider students' grade levels, at-risk conditions and behaviors, i.e., learning difficulties, substance abuse, or lack of social skills. Second, ask students to suggest field trips they think will be beneficial. Third, compile a list of possible field trips for elementary and middle school students and provide a rationale, especially for learners at-risk.

Homework

One teacher of students at-risk told us, "Why give them homework? They won't do it anyway! That's why they are at-risk." This is a mindset that we do not want readers to adopt. Also, such an opinion ignores the fact that learners at-risk can be intelligent, motivated, and conscientious learners, and still be at-risk of sexual experimentation or drug and alcohol abuse. The academically successful student might complete homework assignments to perfection and abuse drugs and alcohol at the same time. All professionals need to avoid falling into the trap of considering that all learners at-risk will not complete homework assignments.

Homework assignments, when properly done, can have several advantages. Homework assignments can serve to reinforce concepts studied in class, provide opportunities for students to work independently and to develop responsibility, and can provide a chance for parents to get involved. Advantages will vary depending on the child's age—a student in the lower elementary grades might be more enthusiastic toward doing homework than students in grades 6-8. Likewise, parents might be more involved (thus, holding them more accountable) with younger children than older children. The type, amount, and difficulty of the homework deserve to be considered with respect to both the maturity of the learner as well as the specific at-risk condition or behavior.

Although students sometimes fail to complete homework assignments, it has been our experience that most students will do homework assignments when teachers meet several conditions. First, teachers need to look for the reason for students failing to do homework assignments—the only way is to know the *individual* student and his or her at-risk condition or behavior. One should question why a capable and motivated student does not complete homework assignments.

Second, teachers need to know (and plan accordingly) for the learning disabled or other academically disabled student who might not be able to complete the homework. Third, teachers need to determine whether homework might be too lengthy, difficult, and time consuming. Fourth, teachers need, whenever possible, to make homework relevant to students' lives, thus contributing to them seeing a reason for doing assignments. Fifth, teachers need to check homework everyday, so students will know it is taken seriously. It might not be necessary to give each homework assignment a grade, but teachers should in some way let learners know they are accountable for out-of-class assignments.

Individualized Instruction

Instruction is most effective when students receive individualized or personalized attention. Methods and strategies designed to individualize 1) assume the belief that children are unique and differ in abilities, motivation, and at-risk conditions and behaviors; 2) assess each learner's unique weaknesses and strengths; 3) provide instructional experiences that meet students' developmental level, learning level, and specific at-risk conditions and behaviors; and 4) assess individual progress using evaluative criteria that determine his or her progress rather than comparing the student to a group norm. One of the greatest advantages of individualized instruction is that the teacher tailors instruction precisely to a particular student's strengths and weaknesses. If the student learns quickly, the teacher can move to other learning tasks; if the student needs more attention, the teacher can try to determine the problem, experiment with other methods and techniques, and spend additional time on the task. Methods and Strategies 3.5 suggests how educators can individualize instruction.

✔ Methods and Strategies 3.5: Understanding Ways to Individualize Instruction

Based upon students' individual development, interests, abilities, and specific at-risk conditions and behaviors, try the following methods of individualizing instruction: peer-tutoring, learning contracts, programmed instruction, team-assisted individualization, and computer-assisted instruction. Undoubtedly, perceptive readers can think of other methods as well as list the advantages and disadvantages of each.

Although individualized instruction is probably the most effective means of teaching, the problem of time prevents its use. Most teachers, unless they have a class of less than six or seven, will experience difficulty finding time and energy to provide individual instruction. Even with a class of six or seven, the teacher would be challenged to find the time to do all the tasks required for genuine individualization. Based on the reality of this situation, teachers can resort to several instructional alternatives that contribute to individualized instruction:

- With programmed instruction, students work on self-instructional materials at their own levels and rates.
- In team-assisted individualization, students work on individualized self-instructional materials at their own levels and rates.
- Peer tutoring allows work in tutoring situations, i.e., a learner in the sixth grade may help a third-grade learner.
- Computer-assisted instruction allows students opportunities to use tutorial programs, problem-solving programs, and dialogue programs.

Expository Teaching

In expository teaching, the teacher acts as a director of instruction. In this traditional method of teaching, the teacher acts to convey content information to learners in a direct, concise, and time-efficient manner. Teachers present lessons in a predetermined sequence and on predetermined schedules. Expository teaching strategies are geared toward direct instruction and include lecture, videos, reading from a textbook or tradebook, demonstration, or computer software (Jarolimek & Foster, 1989). This type of teaching can be harmful to learners at-risk when teachers have too many students in the class, fail to realize the need for determination of students' individual strengths and weaknesses, or teach to the entire class, thus failing to personalize instruction. Still, even with these pitfalls, expository teaching can be beneficial when used in a manner that reflects the nature and needs of learners at-risk.

Using expository teaching, teachers can plan precisely what they want to do in a predetermined sequence, and while problem-free plans do not exist, they feel expository teaching does not have the problems often associated with other instructional methods and strategies. They feel they have more control over the teaching-learning situation—students are often (but not always) listeners or recipients of information. In essence, they feel "less can go wrong" with expository teaching. While we realize that some information is best conveyed through expository teaching, we believe teachers should make accommodations for learners at-risk who might lack the ability to concentrate for long periods of time or who might be more productively engaged with other types of instruction such as more individualized approaches.

Learning Centers

A learning center is a special station located in the classroom where one or two (perhaps more, depending on the design of the center) can quietly work and learn more about a topic at his or her own pace, reinforce learning, or improve specific skills. The center includes all materials and instructions, so students can also work independently. The value of the learning center lies in its instructional diversity. While working at the center, learners are giving time and attention to the learning task and are likely to be engaging their most effective learning strategies. To adapt instruction to students' individual needs and preferences, teachers can design a number of centers, each accommodating particular student needs. While the primary reason for the learning center is to individualize (e.g., provide collections of materials and activities adjusted to various readiness levels, interests, and learning profiles), other reasons include: 1) a means of learning across curricular boundaries; 2) a place for a student with special learning needs and interests; 3) opportunities for creative work and enrichment experiences; and 4) opportunities to learn from learning packages that utilize special equipment that might be limited in supply (Kellough & Kellough, 1999). Methods and Strategies 3.6 explains several considerations for planning learning centers.

Methods and Strategies 3.6:
Understanding Essentials of Learning Centers

When planning learning centers, keep several considerations in mind:
1. Activities should cater toward the needs of learners at-risk and their specific conditions and behaviors.

2. Activities should address both cognitive and affective domains.
3. Activities should address individual differences as much as possible.
4. Activities should provide a method of checking and recording progress.
5. Activities should be "time-efficient" where students do not spend too much time on "mechanics."
6. Activities should be self-explanatory and require only a minimum amount of teacher direction.
7. Activities should have a clear rationale that students can easily understand.

Peer Tutoring

Peer tutoring, as the name implies, is when one student tutors another. Students can sometimes explain a concept or skill better than the teacher, since learners at-risk can often understand another student's perspective. Selected examples of peer tutoring include one student helping a student experiencing reading difficulties, a student who has difficulty understanding a mathematics concept, or a student who needs additional explanations. Usually peer-tutoring occurs within the same class, but, occasionally, students from one grade level tutor students in another grade level. For peer tutoring to be effective, it requires far more than just asking one student to help another.

Peer tutoring frees up the teacher to work with other students, promotes socialization among cultures and both genders, and reinforces the tutor's skills. At least one precaution should be heeded—educators do not want to take the tutor away from her or his own learning to an extent that her or his own progress suffers. One teacher we know keeps a detailed chart of peer tutors, with their expertises, and how much they have tutored, so she always knows the amount of time each tutor has spent away from her or his own studies. For peer tutoring to be successful, teachers need to teach peer tutors how to tutor, attitudes to take, how to encourage, and how to motivate.

Role Playing

Role playing can be particularly helpful when teaching learners at-risk. Some learners, depending on their at-risk behavior or condition, might need to role play the student experimenting with drugs and the adult trying to get him or her to stop; the student applying for a part-time job and the necessity of being on time, the importance of dress and manners, and other aspects often necessary for getting a job; and the boy or girl trying to resist peer pressure and the person trying to get him or her to engage in an at-risk behavior. Other more "academic" role playing situations include a scientist, a person in history, or an author dealing with a controversial subject.

Teachers cannot assume students, at-risk or otherwise, know how to role play. They might have to be taught how to take another's perspective, how to be convincing and realistic, and how to determine what aspects might be raised during the role play. Manners, constructive criticism (both giving and accepting), and "rules" of the role play might have to be taught. Regardless of the work involved in teaching students how to role play, we have seen this method work with learners at-risk, especially students engaging in risky behaviors such as sexual experimentation, substance abuse, and other dangerous behaviors. Methods and Strategies 3.7 suggests various role playing situations for learners at-risk.

✔ ## Methods and Strategies 3.7: Suggesting Various Role Playing Situations for Learners At-Risk

Role play several situations that might prove particularly effective with learners at-risk. For example, role play 1) a conflict or disagreement between two students about a lunchroom incident; 2) a situation between the teacher and a student about an incomplete homework assignment; 3) a parent-child discussion over possible substance abuse; and 4) an eighth grade student interviewing with a potential employer for a part-time job.

Providing Appropriate Assessment.

As with many students, learners at-risk might feel threatened by assessment. Such a belief does not mean we think assessment should be eliminated. Quite the contrary, we think assessment can serve useful purposes such as diagnosing strengths, weaknesses, and areas of interest; reporting progress to the various constituencies; and determining student learning/teacher effectiveness. We also think assessment formats should reflect the needs and uniquenesses of learners at-risk.

Challenges to Learners At-Risk

Assessment often receives harsh criticism, especially from those who feel grading negatively affects students. They feel assessment causes learner stress for both learners and teachers, takes a toll on self-esteem, and fails to take into account learners' many individual differences. For learners at-risk especially, assessment devices might measure only weaknesses instead of strengths and may unfairly place the learner at-risk. Also, realistically speaking, assessment has long been used for reporting progress to students, parents, administrators, and other interested parties and with the current demands for accountability, will probably continue into the future. Therefore, professional educators have a responsibility to accept assessment and to use its advantages, i.e., its potential to diagnose learning problems as well as special strengths and interests. Since assessment will continue, the key for educators will be to understand the criticisms and to minimize the negative effects. Methods and Strategies 3.8 suggests how teachers can talk with learners at-risk about assessment.

✔ Methods and Strategies 3.8:
Talking With Learners At-Risk About Assessment

Discuss with a group of elementary or middle school students how they feel about testing and assessment: What are their opinions of testing? Does it cause stress? How does testing make them feel? Do they feel threatened? What types of assessment do they like best? What would they like to change about testing?

Useful Purposes—Diagnosing, Assessing Progress, and Reporting

Assessment should be a planned and continuous process that diagnoses problems as well as reports to parties interested in learners' progress. While assessment has received considerable criticism, it can also play a major role in identifying learners' strengths, weaknesses, and progress. Effective assessment can provide teachers with an indication of student progress toward learning objectives, of tasks that need to be re-taught or reinforced, and of the most effective teaching methods.

Diagnostic assessment can provide valuable information about reasons for learning problems and for lack of motivation. Diagnostic assessment mainly determines individual strengths and weaknesses in an effort to identify those students needing remediation or other special help.

Reporting student progress is another way educators use assessment. Such assessment can be used at any point to show student progress toward learning goals, whether set by the teacher, the school district, or the state. Again, this oft-criticized assessment can play valuable roles in helping students learn as well as letting parents know how they can assist in the educational process.

Selected Assessment Formats

As previously stated, we think educators should use assessment formats that refect the needs and uniquenesses of learners at-risk. While many undoubtedly exist (depending to some extent on teachers' creativity), two that we think have potential include 1) simulations and role playing and 2) portfolio assessment. Both these devices lsssen the likelihhod that learners at-risk will be faced with essay questions, multiple choice, completion, and true-false test items.

Simulations are replications of real events. Learners engaged in role playing assume the position of another person and use one's own knowledge and skill to act as the person might act. A simple simulation is to give students a social or other learning situation to role play, perhaps from more than one perspective. A teacher might ask a student or a group of students to role play a curator of a museum. Students, then, design and defend the need for and interest in an exhibit on colonial life. Students might role play tour guides and design a tour itinerary featuring the architectural highlights of the school building (Dana & Tippins, 1993).

Portfolios, currently a popular approach to evaluation, allow teachers to evaluate work that students have collected over a period of time rather than just on a few selected days. Portfolio assessment is based on a systematic, purposeful, and meaningful collection of student work that exhibits the student's overall effort, progress, and achievements in one or more subject areas. Portfolio contents can range from paper and pencil tests to creative writing pieces and drawings or graphs (Schurr, 1998). Portfolios allow students to demonstrate what they learned over a period of time rather than at several specific points of time during a grading period.

Portfolios can include a wide variety of work samples selected by the student, parent, peer, and/or the teacher. It is important that portfolios be ongoing and reflect the daily learning activities of the student over time. An important element of all portfolios is the self-reflection piece, which requires the student to analyze his or her own work samples. Portfolios can include several different types of work samples, such as essays, reports, letters, creative writing, problem statements and solutions, journal entries, interviews, artistic media, collaborative works, workbook pages and tests, surveys and questionnaires, reading lists and reviews, self-assessment checklists and statements, teacher checklists and comments, peer reviews, or parent observation and comments (Schurr, 1998).

Portfolios are increasingly popular assessment tools because (Schurr, 1998):
- They are tools for discussion.
- They provide opportunities for students to demonstrate what they know and what they do.
- They provide a vehicle for students to reflect on their work.
- They document the growth of students over a period of time.
- They cater to alternative student learning styles and multiple intelligences.
- They allow students to make decisions about what to include or exclude.
- They make it easier for students to make connections between prior knowledge and new learning.

Summary

Learners at-risk undoubtedly need methods, strategies, and assessment that meet their developmental and learning needs as well as their respective at-risk conditions and behaviors. Likewise, their multiple intelligences, learning styles, and other learning differences should form the basis for selecting methods and strategies. However, educational experiences for learners at-risk should include more than just the cognitive areas. Teachers also need to address learners' affected areas such as how to socialize and get along with others, how to work with others cooperatively and collaboratively, how to deal with peer pressure, and how to cope or deal with specific at-risk conditions or behaviors.

Overall, we think the key to effective methods and strategies for learners at-risk is to diagnose specific conditions and behaviors and, then, plan instruction accordingly. As one teacher we know summed up the challenge, "That's an awfully difficult task; but when I can do it, it usually helps the students, and that's my goal."

Additional Information and Resources

Burnet, D. (1999). Top ten points about being a continuous learner. Burnet offers insightful points about people engaging in continuous learning. http://www.thelearningcoach.com/10topcontinlearner.html

Carbo, M. (1997). Learning style strategies that help at-risk students read and succeed. *Reaching Today's Youth: The Community Circle of Caring, 1*(2), 37–42. Carbo provides an array of teaching strategies that have proven successful with learners at-risk.

Gan, S. L. (1999). Motivating at-risk students through computer-based cooperative learning activities. *Educational HORIZONS 77*(3), 151–156.

Institute for Learning and Communication Strategies. (1999). This internet site provides valuable information on authentic instructional practices, roles of educators, and responding to diverse learners. http://www.learncom.org/advanced/adv-lrn.html

Silver, H., Strong, R., & Perini, M. (1997). Integrating learning styles and multiple intelligences. *Educational Leadership, 55*(1), 22–27. These authors look at learning styles and multiple intelligences and explain how to enhance the strengths of each, thus improving educational experiences.

Sprenger, M. (1999). *Learning and memory: The brain in action* (Alexandria, VA: Association for Supervision and Curriculum Development.) In her comprehensive examination of brain research, Sprenger provides an understandable look at the brain and how educators can provide brain-compatible learning experiences.

Tomlinson, C. A., & Kalbfleisch, M. L. (1998). Teach me, teach my brain: A call for differentiated classrooms. *Educational Leadership 56*(3), 52–55. These authors maintain that three principles from brain research—emotional safety, appropriate challenge, and self-constructed meaning—suggest the need for differentiated instruction.

Chapter 4	# Alternative Learning Environments

Overview

Learners at-risk often need a "different" learning environment, one that differs substantially from what other students consider appropriate for learning. Most schools today still adhere to a formal routine of bells and periods, strict behavior codes with prescribed consequences, and an emphasis on individualism and competition. While such a learning environment might work for some students, other students learn and socialize better in a more relaxed and informal setting. Our experiences have indicated that students at-risk often learn better in "different" or "alternative" environments. They perform better in small, heterogeneous groups, collaborative relationships, and a less structured or hurried schedule. An environment such as we are advocating is best accomplished through team efforts of teachers, administrators, students, and parents. This chapter describes alternative learning environments and suggests steps to implementing environments that might better meet the needs of students at-risk.

Chapter Objectives

After reading and thinking about this chapter on alternative learning environments, the reader should be able to:

1. Define alternative learning environments for learners at-risk and offer a rationale for an environment more conducive to learning.

2. List several characteristics of alternative learning environments.

3. Suggest several worries or concerns that students might have about schools and possible ways to help students cope with school pressures.

4. Explain the need for caring school cultures, especially for students at-risk.

5. Explain the importance of positive learning environments and suggest several ways of accomplishing this goal.

6. List several steps to implementing alternative learning environments.
7. Explain the importance of collaborative team efforts of teachers, administrators, parents, and students.
8. Explain the necessity of tracking progress toward alternative learning environments for learners at-risk and educators' commitment to such a goal.

Alternative Learning Environments for Learners At-Risk

Definition

The learning environment is the overall perception of how students consider the school—its teachers, rules and regulations, both spoken and implied expectations, and the various factors that influence how students feel about the school. Students sometimes view school learning environments as harsh, punitive, and negative. Instead of their successes being celebrated, their failures and shortcomings are emphasized. In some overcrowded schools, students feel rushed through the routine of classes, lunch, and co-curricular activities. Unmotivated and learning challenged students often feel neglected and perceive schools as a place that puts students in "winning" and "losing" situations. Some students do not experience school success in these environments that they perceive as impersonal, punitive, and unresponsive. They experience greater school success (i.e., increased academic achievement, improved socialization, and better behavior) with a learning environment that differs from what we just described.

Working toward a positive school climate means that dedicated individuals make conscious efforts to enhance and enrich the culture and conditions in the school, so that teachers can teach better and students can learn more (Hansen & Childs, 1998).

We define an alternative learning environment as one that provides a sense of positiveness and genuine caring, treats students as individuals, builds upon students' interests and strengths, emphasizes collaboration and group work, provides fewer rules and greater expectations for responsible behavior, and addresses individuals' learning and socialization needs. In essence, we want a nurturing school environment where all individuals are valued and where people feel respected and nurtured, with everyone accepting responsibility for student success.

Because students at-risk may feel alienated from school, educators need to make school a more supportive place. Some features of supportive school environments include self-esteem improvement, teachers' modeling appropriate behaviors, limited class size, teachers who want to work in facilitative environments, avoidance of traditional rewards and punishments, and an emphasis on trust, respect, and cooperation (Conant, 1992). The school climate where teachers can teach more effectively and students can develop more positive self-images includes a safe and orderly learning environment, a clear educational mission, effective instructional leadership, a strong home-school partnership, and high student expectations (Richardson, 1993).

Both students and teachers benefit when school environments focus on the positive. Many students at-risk feel better able to learn and cope in an alternative learning environment—they feel more secure, more confident of their abilities, and more capable of succeeding at school tasks. Also, teachers often perceive the benefits of a more student-centered learning environment. At one school we visit, the teachers hoped such an environment would lessen conflicts between educators and students, reduce discipline referrals, and reduce confrontations among students. By eliminating the "students versus educators" mentality, they hoped students would perceive the harmonious relationships in the school and see less need to engage in hostile and confrontational behaviors. While their efforts focused on the entire student body, we are referring only to students at-risk and how educators can provide an alternative learning environment that will better meet their needs.

Characteristics

Characteristics of effective alternative learning environments include an attention to individual needs, a caring school culture, and small communities of learning.

Characteristic 1—Addressing Individual Needs. What might educators do to incorporate organizational strategies and instructional methods that enhance alternative learning environments? While ideas are limited only by teachers' creativity and commitment, several come to mind such as addressing specific at-risk behaviors and conditions, and providing curricular, instructional, and organizational experiences that reflect students' strengths and interests.

Some people think all learners at-risk can be placed, both figuratively and literally, in one group. "They are all basically alike—let's group them altogether," we heard one teacher say. Such an assertion assumes all learners at-risk share similar problems and characteristics, when in fact, they differ significantly with regard to types of at-risk behaviors and conditions as well as degrees of severity. Therefore, the tremendous diversity among learners at-risk prevents teachers from assuming too much homogeneity. An intelligent and high achieving student at-risk of experimenting with marijuana is quite different than the learner who is at-risk of failing academically. It makes little sense to put these two students in the same group. The high achiever needs a substance abuse program; the learner failing academically needs his or her own specialized program. Methods and Strategies 4.1 suggests ways of determining needs of individual learners at-risk.

Methods and Strategies 4.1: Determining Needs of Individual Learners At-Risk

Ways to determine the needs of individual learners include:

1. Confer with the individual student and ask what he or she thinks the condition or behavior is—realize he or she might not disclose pertinent information until rapport and trust are developed.
2. Speak to the student's parents or guardians to determine their opinions of conditions or behaviors.
3. Administer an appropriate assessment device (i.e., a diagnostic test or assessment scale) to make the most accurate determination of the individual's at-risk condition or behavior.
4. Meet with community organizations, social services, and law enforcement agencies to determine information that they can legally and professionally share.
5. Ask appropriate school specialists (i.e., IEP specialists, psychologists, guidance counselors, and learning disability specialists) to meet with the student and offer their professional opinions.
6. Meet individually with the student at least once a month to determine whether conditions and behaviors have changed and whether educational experiences need to be altered.

An alternative learning environment for students at-risk should be unique to the school. We do not feel a "canned environmental package" is possible; neither do we think teachers should use an "one-size-fits-all" approach. Still, we want to offer several characteristics of an alternative learning environment that we feel address the needs of students at-risk. Table 4.1 provides examples of characteristics of alternative learning environments that often prove effective with students at-risk.

Table 4.1—Characteristics of Alternative Learning Environments

Alternative learning environments

1. *Provide different educational experiences rather than "more of the same," especially for learners at-risk who have not been successful with traditional school environments.*
2. *Emphasize trust, respect, mutual obligation, and concern for others' welfare.*
3. *Improve verbal environments—less criticism and more praise.*
4. *Implement more positive and less abrasive discipline policies.*
5. *Recognize cultural and gender concerns, i.e., preferences for collaboration and group work rather than individualism and competition.*

---

6. Implement ways to integrate new students into the mainstream of school life to avoid students feeling "lost" or anonymous.
7. Provide opportunities to learn and interact in humane, respectful, and psychologically safe learning environments.
8. Place priority on student-centeredness and demonstrate a sense of collaboration among students and educators.
9. Promote harmony and interpersonal relations among students.
10. Encourage students to feel free to express opinions.
11. Support others in a nonthreatening situation.
12. Emphasize high expectations (realizing everyone will not experience equal success) for academic achievement and behavior.

Jerome Freiberg (1998) also believes that "no single factor determines a school's climate" (p. 22). He did a survey of fifth and sixth graders to determine students' worries about school. We think the results of his survey provide indications of factors educators need to consider in the development of alternative learning environments, particularly environments that are positive and address student concerns and worries. Table 4.2 provides a list of children's worries about school.

Table 4.2—Children's Worries About School

Students Entering Middle School

Worry	Worried/Very Worried
Being sent to principal's office	51.77%
Failure	50.19%
Drugs	43.53%
Taking tests	43.53%
Giving a presentation in front of others	39.06%

Adapted from:Freiberg, H. J. (1998). Measuring school climate. *Educational Leadership 56*(1), 22–26.

The worries presented in table 4.2 might be particularly acute for students at-risk.

Based upon Freiberg's findings, what might teachers do to change the school environment to lessen these worries and concerns, especially for students at-risk?

- Teach students common reasons for students at-risk being sent to the principal's office and teach them learning and behavior strategies that will reduce the "need" for being sent—emphasize high expectations for both behavior and learning.
- Provide educational experiences that reflect students' learning abilities and developmental levels as well as build upon students' strengths and interests to reduce the chance of failures.
- Provide developmentally appropriate drug education programs designed to teach students at-risk about peer pressure and the dangers of drugs.
- Teach test-taking strategies; make sure students are adequately prepared for tests; and provide alternative assessment devices, whenever possible, that reduce the stress usually associated with traditional assessment and testing methods.
- Teach students to make effective oral presentations, i.e., emphasize self-esteem and confidence in speaking situations—also, allow students to present to one person, a small group, a larger group, and eventually to the entire group.

Characteristic 2—Provides Caring School Culture. Kent Peterson and Terrence Deal (1998) define school culture as "the underground stream of norms, values, beliefs, traditions, and rituals that has built up over time as people work together, solve problems, and confront challenges" (p. 28). This set of expectations and values shape how people think, feel, and act in schools. Schools with strong, positive cultures include staff with a shared sense of purpose; underlying norms of collegiality, improvement, and hard work; rituals and traditions celebrate student accomplishment, teacher innovation, and parent commitment; and success, joy, and humor abound. Strong positive cultures are also places with a shared sense of what is important, a shared sense of ethos and caring and concern, and shared commitment to help students learn (Peterson & Deal, 1998).

While a sense of caring school culture is important for all students, it might be even more important for students at-risk, those students who often need more support, caring, and individual attention. For example, a caring school culture for students at-risk should include students knowing teachers want to work with them, understand at-risk problems and conditions, understand ways to address individual needs, and realize the importance of more cooperation, less punishments, and more small group instruction.

Characteristic 3—Builds Small Communities of Learning. Especially for learners at-risk, we prefer smaller communities of learning where students and teachers feel a sense of togetherness and know each other sufficiently well to create a climate for intellectual development, shared educational purpose, and appropriate socialization. In other words, a community should be a small, heterogeneous group of students who work collaboratively in an atmosphere of respect and caring. Such organizational practices can result in an alternative learning environment in which students develop a "sense of community."

In communities of learning designed for learners at-risk, students feel less anonymous—they are members of a smaller group and experience a sense of unity with others that a large group might not allow. They get to know others on a more personal basis. Also, working with smaller groups in an atmosphere of caring and respect, teachers can give students more "individualized" time.

As readers might expect, challenges can hinder the development of a sense of community. Methods and Strategies 4.2 looks at several possible challenges and strategies for addressing the challenges.

Methods and Strategies 4.2:
"Community"—Challenges and Strategies

Building a sense of "community" can lead to several challenges; however, remedies to lessen the conflict do exist.

1. Teachers sometimes feel "community" conflicts with traditional values such as achievement and competition.

    Strategy for addressing the challenge: Emphasize "community" can be more productive in terms of achievement and relationships.

2. Teachers sometimes feel "communities" become exclusionary (Westheimer & Kahne, 1993).

    Strategy for addressing the challenge: Prevent cliques by building firm identities within "communities" (Graves, 1992).

3. Teachers sometimes consider "community" a diversion from school purpose or assume community feelings develop automatically.

    Strategy for addressing the challenge: Explain similarities among "schools" and "communities" and how each complements the other.

While Schaps and Lewis (1998) wrote mainly of promoting citizenship through school communities, their points apply to our perception of how communities of learning should be formed. First, they contend that communities need a deep regard and appreciation for self and others. Second, community members should be committed to the core values of justice, caring, fairness, honesty, kindness, responsibility, and compassion. Third, members strive to be civil and considerate in their interactions with others, both in their values and actions.

How can a sense of community be achieved? First, it is important to say that we feel developing a sense of community is a *process rather than a product*. Teachers and students probably will not be able to say the job of developing such a community is completed—it will continue to progress (and at times, probably take a step backwards), and will change as teachers and students develop a sense of caring for each other. Still, Schaps and Lewis (1998) listed several practical directions for educators:

- Regular class meetings in which students shape classroom expectations and practices.
- Opportunities for students and teachers to get to know one another as people and to build a sense of unity, by creating class traditions, class books, and other collaborative projects.
- Disciplinary approaches that foster the desire to do what is right and engage students in active self-improvement, rather than relying only on rewards and sanctions.
- Collaborative learning that emphasizes challenging academics and respectful treatment of other students.
- Curricula that engage students in studying issues that focus on what it means to be a principled, compassionate person.

Characteristic 4—Providing Positive Learning Environments. Positive learning environments offer more collaboration and less competition, fewer rules rather than more, more freedom and accompanying responsibility, positive consequences and reinforcement rather than emphasizing "punishments," and heterogeneous grouping rather than grouping students by ability.

Promoting Civility

Writing about incivility and promoting civility, Victor Scott (1998) maintaines that at a time when single-parent families and families with two working parents are the norm, educators continue to focus on cognitive development and leave affective domains to the family, neighborhood, counselors, and community volunteers. Problematic consequences often result: Students do not learn constructive and productive use of spare time, maintain a healthy lifestyle, and practice personal hygiene. Bells and whistles add confusion to an already disjointed curriculum that does little to teach students how to get along with themselves and others. Methods and Strategies 4.3 suggests ways educators of students at-risk can encourage "civility."

 ## *Methods and Strategies 4.3:*
Encouraging Civility

Educators of students at-risk can encourage "civility" in several ways:

1. Focus educational efforts toward both cognitive *and* affective domains.
2. Change the school day from the traditional "periods" to a more flexible school day (i.e., change from 50 minute periods to a more flexible schedule).

3. Provide times for students to socialize, eat a healthy lunch, and practice hygiene.

4. Teach students how to use their leisure time productively and acceptably.

5. Provide age-appropriate discussions on drug abuse, sex, and violence.

6. Structure the school day to lessen emotional and physiological stress.

7. Teach students how to think and act in restrooms, hallways, locker rooms, and lunchrooms.

Developed from: Scott, V. (1998). Breaking the cycle of incivility. *The High School Magazine*, 6(1), 4–7.

Teaching students how to act appropriately and holding students accountable speaks louder than any after-the-fact disciplinary action. Teenagers who think and act appropriately outside the classroom will continue to do so when they enter the classroom, creating a cycle of positive behavior (Scott, 1998).

Lessening Competition and Providing Cooperation and Collaboration

American schools traditionally have emphasized competition and in some cases, relied on competition to motivate students. The idea was that students wanted to do "better" than others, whether in athletics or academics. Educators thought students competing with others resulted in higher academic achievement—thus excelling at the expense of others created a sense of satisfaction and personal achievement. Proponents of achievement also thought lower achievers would be motivated to "catch up" with faster, more successful students.

While some students (perhaps the more successful) might have benefitted from competition, most educators now agree that many students did not benefit, and in fact, would have achieved more from cooperative and collaborative settings. Many learners at-risk fall into this category. Either due to lower self-esteem or low academic abilities or some combination, they feel frustrated, inadequate, and, unable to compete with others. Plus, some simply do not like to compete—they do not want to excel at the expense of their peers and they do not want to "stand apart" from their friends. In essence, they benefit more from working collaboratively and cooperatively in a climate where others offer and receive help.

Effective programs for students at-risk often include peer tutoring, cooperative learning, and small group work. The emphasis is on positive relationships where some students do not feel like "losers" or "failures." In these programs, hard feelings do not result from some students winning and others losing. To achieve such a learning climate, educators often have to change their mindsets toward the benefits of competition and replace competitive efforts with collaborative efforts. We believe such actions will improve self-esteem and academic achievement for students at-risk as well as improve the overall learning environment.

Providing Fewer Rules and Consequences

J. Merrell Hansen and John Childs (1998) contended that schools some-times appear arbitrary, autocratic, and insensitive. Although rules and regula-tions are necessary, sometimes they exist because of tradition and ritual rather than because they promote or encourage an effective school.

Educators of students at-risk should take systematic and deliberate action to provide fewer rules and more positive consequences. Rather than believing more rules, "get-tough" policies, and stricter suspension and expulsion prac-tices are the answer, many educators recognize that the problems demand more comprehensive solutions. Such a belief does not suggest students at-risk should be given more freedom than they can handle; neither does it mean teachers should not have high expectations for students' behavior. However, alternative learning environments that meet the developmental, academic, and social needs of students often provide more freedom than traditionally expected.

Our preservice teachers often question our belief that students often be-have better with fewer rules than with a longer or more comprehensive list. However, in many of the programs we visit, teachers allow considerable free-dom—they have fewer rules and allow students more freedom, yet they con-tinue to expect students to model appropriate behavior and accept responsibil-ity for inappropriate behaviors. In situations with fewer rules, students feel teachers trust them more and expect them to be sufficiently responsible to be-have in an acceptable manner. Case Study 4.1 illustrates the point that students might behave better when they have fewer rules.

Case Study 4.1:
 ## Mrs. Carlson's Rules and Regulations

Mrs. Carlson, a sixth grade teacher, had many detailed rules, and students always knew exactly what they were allowed to do and not allowed to do. The rules and the consequences were specifically spelled out. Students were ruled with an "iron fist"—they knew the limits and realized the consequences for breaking the rules. Students competed—both for Mrs. Carlson's time as well with each other for grades. Since educational experiences were competitive in nature, collaboration and cooperation were taboo. Believing students should be grouped by ability, Mrs. Carlson advocated homogeneous grouping. Even with this seemingly controlled organization, Mrs. Carlson experienced "problems"—some students still tried to find a way to misbehave (yet without breaking a rule); they bickered among themselves, and, generally speaking, students ap-peared disgruntled.

When she asked the Collaborative Team Committee for advice, she was expecting them to suggest more stringent rules, more punishments, and disci-pline referrals. Instead, she was surprised when several members referred to the "fewer classroom rules—better student behavior" belief. They suggested she try fewer rules and heterogeneous grouping for awhile. Last, they cajoled her to develop trust in her students, to show the students the respect that she demanded of them, and to at least try to develop a positive climate. While a bit skeptical, she felt the advice was at least worth a try.

Ensuring Positive Reinforcement

In their hurried day, teachers too often assume students know academic and behavioral successes. "Students know when they make a good grade; they know when they behave," we heard one teacher say. While we agree to some extent, we still feel that teachers, especially teachers of students at-risk, should provide positive reinforcement for good grades, commendable effort, and appropriate behavior. The use of positive reinforcement can apprise students of their successes or their progress toward acceptable achievement and behavior. It can serve as an excellent means of encouragement and can serve as a motivating device.

Grouping Heterogeneously

Grouping students on the basis of achievement level and academic ability (e.g., standardized achievement tests, teacher-made tests, previous teachers' recommendations) has been an integral part of American education (Vaughn, Bos, & Schumm, 1997). Recently, there has been increased support for heterogeneous or "mixed-ability" grouping. Heterogeneous learning can be defined as educators organizing students into groups without regard to academic ability and expertise, intelligence, and previous learning achievement.

Several points deserve to be mentioned as teachers group students at-risk heterogeneously. First, students at-risk, should not feel like second-class citizens and should not be subject to self-fulfilling prophecies of failure, both attributed to homogeneous grouping. Second, similarities and differences exist within heterogeneous groups that can be addressed though appropriate use of mastery learning, individualized instruction, peer tutors, and cooperative learning. Third, it is still possible to organize students at-risk with others of similar abilities, interests, and areas of expertise. The difference is that teachers do not form fixed groups where students feel penalized for lack of academic or social abilities. Methods and Strategies 4.4 suggests ways to address student diversity.

Methods and Strategies 4.4:
Addressing Student Diversity

Educators wanting to address a wide range of student abilities can use:

1. A wide range of organizational arrangements such as multiage grouping, developmental age grouping, and alternate schedules.
2. Peer tutors to help slower students—peer tutors can be excellent sources of motivation, may be able to explain concepts on another student's level, and provide one-on-one help that teachers might not have time to provide.

3. Learning contracts, as discussed in chapter 2, where students can "con-tract" for the learning objectives, instructional methods, materials, and assessment instruments.

4. Computer programs for remediation and enrichment that serve as a means of individualizing instruction for both slow and more advanced learners.

5. Independent study during which students can work alone on a topic of interest—doing research, reading books on a particular topic, prepar-ing a research paper, and planning the most effective means of presen-tation to the class.

6. Learning centers where three or four students can focus on regular in-struction as well as remedial and enrichment experiences.

7. Tape recordings of content—tapes can be taken home and listened to repeatedly. Tapes can address the needs of students who learn "auditorily" as well as students who just need additional instruction.

Using Positive Verbal Comments

Another factor involved in providing positive learning environments is how students at-risk perceive verbal environments. Negative verbal environ-ments cause learners to feel unworthy, incompetent, or insignificant. The most obvious examples include screaming at or making fun of students. Yet, more common adult behaviors may include showing little or no interest in chil-dren, speaking discourteously, or dominating verbal exchanges that occur daily. Verbal comments in positive environments are aimed at satisfying learners' psychological needs and by making them feel valued. To promote positive environments, teachers should use words that show caring and affection, should plan spontaneous opportunities to talk with each learner, and should avoid making judgmental comments about learners (Kostelnik, Stein, Whiren, & Soderman, 1988).

In a class of seventh graders at-risk that we often visit, the teachers have made a commitment as a group to promote a positive learning environment. Teachers correct students whenever needed and maintain high standards for both achievement and behavior; however, corrections are done in a positive manner. Students are never "put down," made to feel inadequate, or embar-rassed in front of their peers. The emphasis is on being positive, both in terms of actual words as well as demeanors with students. Interestingly, the teachers' modeling of positive behaviors and verbal comments has motivated students (unfortunately, to varying degrees with some) to change to more positive be-haviors. Methods and Strategies 4.5 suggests how educators can encourage positive verbal interactions.

Methods and Strategies 4.5:
Encouraging Positive Verbal Interactions

Teachers wanting a positive verbal environment can:

1. Model verbal responses and interactions that they want others to adopt.
2. Teach students the need for positive verbal comments such as the need to avoid sarcasm and hurtful comments about others' abilities and appearances.
3. Emphasize the need to avoid stereotypical comments and other derogatory remarks about others' cultural backgrounds, gender, socioeconomic class, religions, and sexual orientation.
4. Teach students to speak courteously and to listen attentively, just as they expect to be treated
5. Role play situations that demonstrate positive verbal interactions and responses.

Steps to Implementing Alternative Learning Environments

One school decided to take definite steps to improve the school environment. The educators wanted to determine changes and innovations that held potential for making the school environment more positive. They discussed scheduling, discipline procedures, teaching methods, school organization, guidance programs, and the overall culture of the school. Practicing teachers from other school systems, administrators, and educators worked collaboratively to determine how to make the environment more positive, humane, and caring. Based upon this school's progress, we concluded several steps for implementing alternative learning environments. Methods and Strategies 4.6 shows steps toward alternative learning environments.

Methods and Strategies 4.6:
Steps Toward Alternative Learning Environments

Educators who want to make their school environment more student-centered, collaborative, harmonious, and generally speaking, more positive can take several steps:

1. Form a group of educators who have a genuine commitment to improve the school environment and who will work collaboratively toward group goals.
2. Charge this group with the responsibility of communicating with other faculty members in the school—other educators should always feel they know the group's efforts, understand reasons for decisions, and feel they can offer opinions that will be thoughtfully considered.
3. Involve at least one administrator, two or three parents of learners at-

risk, and perhaps one or two students who understand the importance of school environment on academic achievement and teacher and student relationships.

4. Provide the group with assistance, i.e., other educators who have first-hand experience with improving school environments, either from within the school system or from another school system.

5. Reach consensus (i.e., other educators in the school, students, and parent representatives) on characteristics of an environment that meet students' and educators' needs in the particular school.

6. Decide on specific efforts or programs that hold potential for achieving the characteristics of a positive environment.

7. Assess present school practices and policies to determine changes that hold potential for making the school environment more positive.

8. Realize a positive school environment is a continuing and evolving *process* which can be both frustrating and rewarding.

9. Dream and commit to lofty goals, but avoid too many major simultaneous organizational or instructional changes, so teachers will not be overwhelmed with too many changes at one time.

10. Celebrate accomplishments by taking time to reflect upon what has been achieved.

While these are worthwhile starting points, educators in their respective schools need to consider their existing school environment and determine the type of environment they want.

Collaborative Team Efforts

Individual educators undoubtedly can make significant differences in changing schools to more positive, caring, and humane places; however, team efforts almost always have greater impacts. Implementing alternative learning environments is more than just changing one classroom—it should be a total school approach, one that includes the active involvement of teachers, administrators, parents, and students. Teachers faced with the challenge of addressing the needs of students at-risk can seek advice and support from their colleagues through a variety of collaborative arrangements. Methods and Strategies 4.7 explains directions educators can take to promote collaborative team efforts.

 ## Methods and Strategies 4.7: Collaborative Team Efforts

Educators of students at-risk who choose to work in collaborative teams can take several steps:

1. Design programs and efforts especially for students at-risk.

2. Diagnose specific at-risk behaviors and/or conditions.

3. Monitor student progress—both achievement and behavior.

4. Develop professional expertise to work with students at risk.
5. Work toward effective parent involvement.
6. Address the affective as well as cognitive domains.
7. Provide co-curricular activities that interest and help students at-risk.

A critical need exists for collaborative teams to brainstorm ideas that will meet the needs of students at-risk. Crisis teams, truancy programs, alternative learning centers, a community-based student at-risk committee, and retention-prevention programs are only a few strategies that have potential for helping educators meet student needs and improve student self-image (Richardson, 1993).

Research and Classroom Practice 4.1 examines how educators can implement developmentally responsive learning environments. We think the Clarks' opinions are relevant for educators of students at-risk who undoubtedly need a developmentally responsive learning environment.

Research and Classroom Practice 4.1: Implementing Developmentally Responsive Learning Environments

Donald Clark and Sally Clark, two noted and respected writers, call for principals to be informed, visionary, and collaborative leaders. Effective leadership results when leaders elevate others to higher levels of motivation and effectiveness. These leaders motivate others to follow a higher purpose while taking specific steps to promote the process that brings about meaningful change. Informed leaders, as the term implies, means the principal is informed about all aspects of the school and has the background for convincing teachers, parents, and community members that they have the knowledge and skills to achieve goals. Visionary leaders can see what programs and efforts will be like upon implementation; they have a comprehensive knowledge base that allows them to offer concrete proposals for turning visions into reality. Principals as instructional leaders encourage teachers to examine their belief systems, to consider new ideas, become current in the latest research, and share personal expertise. Collaborative leaders model and encourage collegiality and collaboration—they know collaboration enhances the ability of the school to respond to problems and opportunities as well as increasing effectiveness, efficiency, and productivity.

Source: Clark, D. C., & Clark, S. N. (1998). Creating developmentally responsive learning environments. *Schools in the Middle*, *8*(2), 12–15.

Collaborative teams can contribute to a positive school environment which minimizes the number of students who feel unknown and who feel that teachers do not know their progress in other classes. Teaming helps students build team spirit and improves attitudes and work habits because of the closer, more coherent supervision and caring that occurs on a team. A positive school environment can be developed that emphasizes caring, respect, success, and inter-dependence. Similarly, planning time, materials, and other resources can be shared by professionals.

Tracking Progress and Commitment

In one school we visit, school leaders working to develop and maintain an alternative learning environment realized that expertise and commitments among teachers varied. Therefore, the committee decided on two directions to increase the chances of educational experiences for learners at-risk being implemented effectively.

First, some teachers volunteered to work with teachers who expressed re-luctance. They helped them understand how educational experiences should be implemented by providing them with lesson plans, suggesting ways to use small, collaborative groups more effectively, and recommending techniques for help-ing learners at-risk. Second, the administration implemented accountability measures designed to help teachers. For example, they checked lesson plans, required detailed records of student progress, and monitored discipline refer-rals to determine whether classroom management strategies reflected the needs of students at-risk. Administrators and teacher volunteers conducted direct ob-servations in individual classrooms for the purpose of helping rather than evalu-ating. As with all educational efforts, effective program evaluation is essential. Methods and Strategies 4.8 explains how educators can determine progress and commitment.

Methods and Strategies 4.8: Determining Progress and Commitment

Educators who want to track the progress and commitment to addressing the needs of learners at-risk can ask questions such as:

1. Are there collaborative team efforts (i.e., teachers, library media spe-cialists, administrators, parents, and students) to address the needs of learners at-risk or do only individual teachers exert effort?

2. Are there programs designed for various at-risk conditions and behav-iors or does the school have a "canned or generic program?"

3. Are there carefully designed assessments (i.e., both objective and valid) to determine specific at-risk conditions and behaviors or are assess-ments subjective and subject to error?

4. Are materials purchased or written to address the conditions and be-haviors of students at-risk *in the particular school* or a more general population?

5. Is there a comprehensive program (i.e., instruction, curriculum, alter-native environment, and guidance) or are efforts only piecemeal or haphazard?

6. Is there a carefully-planned program to evaluate the at-risk program or are efforts only superficial?

7. Are there comprehensive efforts to have an alternative learning environment (i.e., a caring culture, a sense of community, and positive verbal comments, or are efforts isolated and of concern to only a few teachers?

Summary

An alternative learning environment can be an influential force in addressing the needs of students at-risk. Effective teachers of students at-risk realize the need to provide different educational experiences rather than more of the same—whether additional worksheets, more drill and practice, or more "programs." An appropriate environment reflects interests and needs of learners at-risk, provides caring school culture, builds small communities of learning, and addresses specific individual at-risk behaviors and conditions. Collaborating in team efforts, teachers also work toward positive learning environments that promote civility, lessen competition and increase cooperation, and, generally speaking, accentuate the positive. While alternative learning environments often require changing mindsets from traditional perspectives of educational practice, we feel the results for students at-risk as well as their teachers is well worth the effort.

Additional Information and Resources

Carroll, P. S., & Taylor, A. (1998). Understanding the culture of the classroom. *Middle School Journal, 30*(1), 9–17. Carroll and Taylor explain a collaborative project and conceptualize the class as a culture.

Hansen, J. M., & Childs, J. (1998). Creating a school where people like to be. *Educational Leadership, 56*(1), 14–17. This article looks at a school that has instilled a positive school climate—positive policies, effective programs, and a participatory process.

Kostelnik, M. J., Stein, L. C., Whiren, A. P., & Soderman, A. K. (1988). *Guiding children's social development*. Cincinnati, OH: Brooks/Cole.

Magna, S. (1999). Creating a classroom culture. Magna explains why classroom cultures are important to educational settings. http://www.ispin.k12.il.us/column3.htm

Schaps, E., & Lewis, C. C. (1998). Breeding citizenship through community in school. *The Education Digest, 64*(1), 23–27. These authors looked at ways to help youth sustain a just and humane democracy and focus specifically on deep regard for self and others as well as core values of justice and caring.

Peterson, K. D., & Deal, T. E. (1998). How leaders influence the culture of
    schools. *Educational Leadership, 56*(1), 28–30. These authors tell about
    four schools that tried to build a positive culture—effective leadership is
    needed to change a school's culture.

Chapter 5

Chapter 5

Classroom Management Techniques and Strategies

Overview

Effective teachers of learners at-risk understand the powerful effects of classroom management beliefs, techniques, and strategies. They base their practices on the philosophy that management has two aspects: 1) teachers accept responsibility for student behavior and 2) teachers accept responsibility for their own teaching behaviors. While we look at the two aspects (i.e., student behavior and teacher behavior) separately, one undoubtedly affects the other. Teachers also realize the need for an effective classroom management system—one that is fair and equitable and one that teaches self-discipline and responsibility for one's behavior. Also, vitally important, the classroom management system—both learners' behaviors and teachers' behaviors—should be developed and implemented with learners at-risk in mind. In this chapter, we look at the management of both learner and teacher behavior and call for management techniques and strategies that reflect the needs of learners at-risk.

Chapter Objectives

After reading and thinking about this chapter on management techniques and strategies, the reader should be able to:

1. Explain how management refers to teachers accepting responsibility for student behavior as well as accepting responsibility for their own teaching behaviors.
2. Identify several considerations for the management of learners at-risk such as environmental and organizational factors, selected special needs of learners at-risk, and characteristics of effective programs.
3. Explain "a sense of community" as a means of providing effective classroom management.
4. Suggest ways to manage special needs learners such as the learning

disabled, emotionally disturbed, attention deficit hyperactive disorder, and limited English proficient.

5. Distinguish between teachers encouraging cooperation and collaboration and teachers establishing rules for strict obedience.

6. Identify effective teaching techniques that research suggests contributes to positive classroom management.

Management—Two Essential Aspects

Some people often associate management with discipline or control. From this perspective, management is something teachers do to students to maintain order or behavior. We see management of learners at-risk as having a broader definition—1) teachers accepting responsibility for student behavior, and 2) teachers accepting responsibility for their own teaching behaviors.

Students' behaviors.

Simply stated, the management of student behaviors is how well teachers promote positive learning environments, maintain order and harmony, build a sense of community, and provide physical and psychological safety. It also includes how teachers perceive behaviors, praise desired behaviors, and correct inappropriate behaviors. This first type of management, that of management of students, refers to the teachers' beliefs and actions to address students' behavior problems or to prevent those problems from occurring. Some teachers we know maintain order through an established set of rules; others have few rules, and order just seems to occur with little effort; and, unfortunately, others yell and threaten, with little positive effect on either the students or the overall classroom climate.

From the perspective of teaching learners at-risk, teachers need to consider at-risk conditions and behaviors and how they might affect behavior. While situations vary, representative examples might include the child with low self-esteem exerting little effort, the learning disabled child feeling frustrated, and the limited English speaking student misbehaving to overcome or compensate for feelings of inadequacy. Methods and Strategies 5.1 looks at several ways teachers can determine reasons for misbehavior.

 ## Methods and Strategies 5.1:
Determining Reasons for Misbehavior

Sometimes, when students misbehave, teachers assume that students are "just bad," or come from home environments that do not promote school efforts. Other more objective ways to determine the causes of student behavior include (Charles, 1999):

*   Do the students feel *inadequate*—do they feel unable to achieve the expected schoolwork or behavior?

- Are the students engaging in *attention-getting*—do they feel they are not getting sufficient teacher or student attention?
- Are the students seeking *power*—do they want to prove they can do whatever they want to do?
- Are the students seeking *revenge*—do they want to hurt and discredit the teacher?

Teachers' Behaviors

The second type of management is how teachers behave as they establish the teaching-learning environment and, generally speaking, interact with students on a daily basis. In this sense, we are seeing teaching as being an integral part of management. Some teachers seem to have excellent management skills and behaviors—they demonstrate confidence; they have high expectations; they know just what to say and when to say it; their teaching objectives and materials reflect learner development and ability; and their students behave and learn. They keep the children on task, use instructional time productively and efficiently, keep students informed of intended objectives, and maintain and convey success expectations for both behavior and academic achievement. Other teachers, a much smaller number we think and hope, demonstrate different behaviors—they seem to struggle through the day as they feel frustrated either with themselves or their students (or both). Their lessons lack smoothness; they lack confidence; they do not believe they can make students behave; and they question their ability to teach. Management is a struggle for both their students and them—neither teachers nor students are at ease and rarely is the teaching-learning experience maximized.

Referring specifically to teachers of learners at-risk, teachers who demonstrate effective management will understand and respond appropriately to learners with shorter attention spans, emotional problems, learning disabilities, problems associated with alcohol and drugs, and other at-risk conditions or behaviors.

Management of Learners At-Risk

The management of learners at-risk includes teachers' efforts to provide a learning environment, classroom organization, and educational programs designed to meet the needs of learners at-risk. What does this mean for teachers of learners at-risk? It means that teachers understand that slightly changed environments, organizations, and programs will not suffice. Instead, teachers consider individual students and their respective at-risk conditions and behaviors and plan all aspects of the school day appropriately.

Environmental and Organizational

The environment and organization of the classroom and school should reflect the needs of learners at-risk as well as their development (i.e., younger children or middle or later childhood). In developing a school environment and organization that is responsive to the needs of learners at-risk, teachers should consider four characteristics.

Characteristic 1—Physically and psychologically safe. While all elementary and middle school students need a physically and psychologically safe class environment, it might be especially important for students at-risk—those students who already might perceive the school as a threatening and harsh place. By physically and psychologically safe, we mean classes, schools, and playgrounds where students feel safe from violence and physical harm. Others are not allowed to pick on or bully them. Likewise, teachers do not allow others to laugh at students because of their names, sizes, cultural backgrounds, and disabling conditions. They also feel safe around teachers—teachers neither yell nor threaten. They treat students with respect and caring concern. They expect students to demonstrate positive behavior toward other students and the teacher. They have high expectations for students, yet they work toward these expectations in positive and humane ways. In other words, students view schools as safe havens, often for some the safest part of their day.

Methods and Strategies 5.2 suggests ways to make classes psychologically safe.

Methods and Strategies 5.2:
Making Classes Psychologically Safe

Suggested ways to make classes psychologically safe include:
1. Show appreciation for students, their individuality, and their efforts.
2. Speak courteously to students and conscientiously listen to their comments.
3. Avoid making harsh and judgmental remarks, sarcasm, and dominating exchanges.
4. Consider students' concerns rather than downplaying their importance.
5. Provide learning experiences that show the affective concerns as well as cognitive concerns.
6. Allow students to help make the classroom rules.
7. At all times, model desired classroom behavior.

Characteristic 2—Effective learning environments. While closely related to characteristic 1, we think it is important to emphasize the importance of effective learning environments. Characteristic 1 considers children feeling safe; characteristic 2 focuses more on *the learning environment*. Also, since alternative learning environments were addressed in chapter 4, it will be examined only briefly here.

An effective learning environment provides learners with programs that:

1) address their individual at-risk behaviors and conditions; 2) provide a positive climate in which students can learn and socialize; 3) provide developmentally responsive educational experiences, i.e., responsive for the age and development of the child; 4) include a teacher who serves as a guide and mentor; and 5) build upon learners' interests and strengths. Books, curricular materials, and software emphasize success rather than penalization for failure. The teacher uses instructional and management methods that promote harmony rather than an "us v. them" attitude.

Characteristic 3—Clear and abbreviated classroom rules. Several experienced teachers of learners at-risk we know emphasize the necessity of clear rules and expectations. In some cases, teachers might have only three or four rules; in others, teachers had eight or so. However, in all cases, the teachers made their expectations for behavior clear, and they carefully explained the reasons for the rules. From the first week of school, students knew the classroom rules and the consequences for breaking the rules. These teachers rarely sent a student to the principal's office or to the guidance counselor—they had few behavior problems and they handled situations within the confines of the classroom. The rules and expectations should reflect the unique needs of learners at-risk, e.g., lower self-esteem, lower abilities, substance abuse, and other at-risk condition or behaviors.

Methods and Strategies 5.3 looks at examples of classroom rules that encompass a wide range of misbehaviors.

Methods and Strategies 5.3: Deciding on Class Rules

While we think teachers should allow and in fact encourage learners to help decide class rules, some examples are (Jones & Jones, 1990):

1. Speak politely to each other.
2. Treat each other kindly.
3. Follow teacher requests.
4. Be prepared for class.
5. Make a good effort at your work and request help if needed.
6. Obey all school rules.

As we mentioned earlier, we feel that sometimes fewer rules result in better behavior. As strange as this might sound, we know classes where a large number of stringent rules resulted in more behavior problems; upon relaxation of the rules, positive behavior increased. One might argue that students accepted greater responsibility for their behavior when they felt they chose the behaviors. This is not to say that students do not need rules and guidelines for their behavior; however, we still believe students often behave better when they accept responsibility for their behavior.

Case Study 5.1 tells about a school's efforts to reduce the number of rules in the hope of improving student behavior.

Case Study 5.1:
Simplifying Discipline Policies

During the fall semester, the educators at a large, urban middle school decided to work toward a positive school environment of trust, respect, mutual obligation, and concern for others' welfare. The educators wanted a school environment that provided students with opportunities to learn and interact in a humane, respectful, and caring learning environment. They wanted a school environment that placed priority on student-centeredness, demonstrated a sense of collaboration among students and educators, promoted harmony and inter-personal relations among students, and reflected positive verbal interactions. Teachers and students needed to feel free to express opinions, listen to others with empathy, and support others in nonthreatening situations. The educators decided the Code of Discipline needed to be simplified and made more positive. The original code allowed administrators and teachers too little flexibility; consequences were listed for infractions without regard for individual circumstances. Students often considered consequences too harsh and teachers felt required to impose consequences rather than teach self-discipline in a positive manner. They thought fewer rules might be better than a longer, detailed list of harsh and punitive consequences. Learners could learn appropriate behavior as well as realize teachers' commitment to positive approaches. The 23 page booklet on rules and regulations for conduct was reduced to a 4 page Code of Discipline. To ensure fair application of the new Code, an appeal process was created for students who felt the rules had not been applied fairly.

Methods and Strategies 5.4 looks at ways educators can re-consider the rules and regulations concerning student behavior.

Methods and Strategies 5.4:
Revisiting Rules of Behavior

Working collaboratively with students, ask their opinions of both classroom and school rules. Then, ask other teachers in the school. Do the students and teachers feel rules are too harsh or too mild? Is the behavior code understandable and about the right length? What school rules should be deleted? What new ones should be added? Is there a consensus among students and teachers that fewer rules usually lead to better student discipline? If the school has a comprehensive and long behavior code, how might it be shortened? What do the students think need to be done for positive behavior to be demonstrated?

Characteristic 4—A sense of community. Although discussed in chapter 4 as a means of providing an alternative learning environment, we believe a sense of community also deserves to be briefly mentioned as a special consideration for effective management of learners at-risk.

Learners at-risk often feel alienated, different, or singled-out due to their conditions and behavior. A sense of community can be particularly beneficial for learners at-risk. Communities focus on social relationships and interdependencies among students and teachers (and parents and families); and communities empower learners and educators and focus on commitments, obligations, and responsibilities that people feel toward each other and toward the school (Sergiovanni, 1994).

Special Considerations

The management of learners at-risk requires consideration of their unique needs and challenges. While individuals should always be considered, some learners at-risk might have shorter attention spans, limited socialization, and differing perspectives toward rules and appropriate behavior.

First, some learners at-risk have shorter attention spans. One of our student teachers said, "They only behave for a few minutes at a time. Their attention is so short that they listen or work for a few minutes and then, start goofing off again." While we agree that some learners at-risk have shorter attention spans, we reminded the student teacher that whether a learner had a shorter attention span depends on the specific at-risk condition or behavior. Teachers can address learners' shorter attention spans in several ways: 1) make sure the educational experiences are on the student's learning and interest levels; 2) change activities every 6-8 minutes (this will, of course, depend on the individual learner); 3) make sure curricular materials are interesting and age-, ability-, and developmentally appropriate; and 4) allow students to work in small groups or other collaborative arrangements. The same student teacher worked with about 8 students—they were about 2-3 feet apart, so they could have "their own space and could not bother others," she stated. We suggested that she try a more flexible room arrangement to see whether students' attention spans might be a little longer if they worked in pairs or two groups of four.

Methods and Strategies 5.5 suggests other ways teachers can address learners' shorter attention spans.

Methods and Strategies 5.5:
Helping Learners With Shorter Attention Spans

1. Teach smaller chunks of information, i.e., expect students to learn less in a given lesson.
2. Make information as relevant as possible—try to relate to learners' lives, both present and future.
3. Allow students to work with a peer tutor, so someone can help them stay on track.
4. Use a number of attention-grabbing devices such as videos, demonstrations, and software.
5. Avoid lecturing or presenting too much material orally.

Second, learners at-risk sometimes lack the socialization skills necessary for acceptable interaction in the classroom, school, and outside world. Learners at-risk sometimes harbor differing perspectives toward rules and appropriate behavior. One teacher we know worked continuously on such mannerisms such as "Good morning," "Excuse me," "May I . . .," and "Thank you." He maintained that learners at-risk in his school often did not know (or did not care about) socially-accepted mannerisms. Also, he did more than just teach these aspects—he daily modeled how they should act and treat others.

A third consideration is that learners at-risk might also have specific special needs such as learning disabilities, emotionally disturbed, attention deficit hyperactive disorder, and limited English proficient.

Learning disabled children sometimes develop behavior problems. They may benefit from keeping a record of their own specific behaviors, including completion of assignments. This helps them build a sense of control over themselves and their environment. Emotionally disturbed learners also provide management challenges. It is important for teachers to avoid taking their lack of cooperation, inappropriate behavior, or verbal attacks personally. When emotionally disturbed students lash out, the teacher might be merely the convenient target rather than the root cause of the problem. Attention-Deficit Hyperactive Disorder (ADHD) children also provide management challenges. Broad characteristics of ADHD learners often include distractibility, short attention spans, impulsiveness, an inability to organize, and a high level of movement. Teachers need to understand that these behaviors are not deliberate and it may take a long time for children to control these behaviors. The numbers of limited English proficiency students continue to increase in elementary and middle schools. Some of these students have acquired sufficient English language skills to perform successfully in English-only classes. Other students have not acquired a sufficient level of skill speaking, understanding, reading, and writing English, and need additional assistance to participate in school activities (Evertson, Emmer, Clements, & Worsham, 1994).

Table 5.1 offers selected suggestions for managing these learners.

Management that Meets the Needs of Learners At-Risk

Effective programs demonstrate an understanding of the characteristics and needs of learners at-risk, i.e., the methods and strategies, the curricular materials, and the overall educational climate are designed *for* learners at-risk and their respective conditions and behaviors. While educators may draw from programs (such as learning goals, teaching methods, and curricular materials) designed for other students, management programs for learners at-risk should not be "watered-down" versions of those offered to other students. One teacher told us she had to be stricter with learners at-risk. "I cannot let them get away with much; they might get out-of-hand," she remarked. We agree with high expectations for both academics and behavior, but we disagree with the belief that teachers should be stricter simply because their learners are placed at-risk.

Table 5.1—Managing Special Needs Learners

Learning Disabled

- Provide positive, structured, and predictable routines.
- Demonstrate considerable patience and provide repetition.
- Help students to identify and give attention to relevant cues and details.
- Emphasize what is correct rather than what is wrong.
- Model appropriate behavior to ensure positive learning rather than reinforcing negative learning.
- Avoid trial and error activities where learners spend too much time on the wrong things.
- Provide opportunities for overlearning since some learners have retention problems.
- Provide shorter practices of tasks over a period of time rather than fewer longer practices.
- Provide multisensory experiences.

Emotionally Disturbed

- Read the psychological report describing these children and note any recommendations.
- Consult with the school psychologist and special education teachers about ways to manage behavior.
- Reinforce all attempts of students to maintain self-control.
- Learn to recognize behavioral cues that may precede an outburst so behavior problems can be anticipated.
- Overlook minor inappropriate behavior, reinforce acceptable behaviors, and reduce stressors.
- Provide a supportive, predictable environment and offer students structured choices.
- Work with administrators and counselors to devise a plan if students have a serious tantrum.
- Provide a safe time-out area to allow students to be separate from other students for a cooling down period of time.

Attention-Deficit Hyperactive Disorder

- Obtain students' attention when giving oral instructions.

- Give brief and clear instructions, preferably one at a time.
- Monitor students as they start new assignments and be willing to state directions individually.
- Adjust the amount of work to reflect students' attention spans.
- Remind students that accuracy is more important than speed.
- Be willing to collect completed assignments since students may lose completed work prior to turning it in.
- Organize the daily schedule so that stimulating or exciting activities come after activities requiring extended concentration.
- Provide a place that is relatively quiet and free of distractions for students who might want to work alone.

Limited English Proficiency Students

- Provide English as a Second Language (ESL) classes to help students learn English as quickly as possible.
- Learn from the ESL or bilingual teacher which students can understand some English and which ones can understand none.
- Learn what children prefer to be called and try to pronounce names correctly.
- Use creativity in communicating, speaking naturally and with pauses and gestures, rather than relying on someone to translate.
- Reinforce key points with visual aids and use clear and concise words.
- Consider using peer buddies who are outgoing and warm to assist with communication and to let students know caring assistance is available even though they are reluctant to speak.

Developed from: Evertson, C. M., Emmer, E. T., Clements, B. S., & Worsham, M. E. (1994). *Classroom management for elementary teachers* (3rd. ed). Boston: Allyn and Bacon, pages 196–199.

First, instead of offering learners at-risk more rules and regulations and "more of the same" educational experiences, teachers need to tailor educational programs to meet the unique needs of individual learners at-risk. For example, the teacher can change activities more often with the student with a short attention span; she or he can work with the guidance counselor to help the student who is being swayed by peer pressure to experiment with illegal substances; and she or he can provide social skills training for students with limited socialization skills or antisocial behavior; and she or he can work toward successful experiences for students who lack self-esteem. In other words, a "one-size-fits-all" program will not work—students differ in their educational goals, learning styles, and types and degrees of at-risk conditions and behaviors.

Research and Classroom Practice 5.1 describes an effort to prevent antisocial behavior in children at-risk.

Research and Classroom Practice 5.1:
First Steps to Prevent Antisocial Behavior

During the past decade, early childhood and primary grade level teachers have been shocked by changes in their students' behavioral characteristics: Not ready to learn, unable to cope with the demands of schooling, unfamiliar with the social tasks involved in making friends and getting along with others, and being unaware of their negative, social impact on others. Many preschoolers and young school-age children routinely display unacceptable behavior: assaults on teachers, physical aggression toward peers, and inappropriate sexual behavior. Some children see violence as a viable means of solving problems, fail to respect the rights of others, demonstrate socially irresponsible behavior, lack basic manners and social conventions, and fail to value human life.

The First Step to Success Program has three components: 1) a universal screening procedure to detect children showing early signs of antisocial behavior; 2) a school intervention to teach the child at-risk adaptive behavior patterns for achieving school success and making friends; and 3) a home component in which parents work as partners with the teacher and school in teaching key skills that contribute to school success. The overall goal of First Step is to help children at-risk get off to the best possible start in school and to divert them from an antisocial path.

The First Step Program works like this: A First Step consultant (e.g., behavioral specialist, early childhood educator, counselor, or school psychologist) initiates and operates the program and, then, turns the school portion over to the classroom teacher. The consultant visits the home for one hour each week and works with the parents on such skills as sharing, accepting limits, cooperation, and self-esteem. The child is followed up and monitored after the completion of the program to preserve achieved behavioral gains. The First Step consultant usually invests 40–50 hours over the course of the program.

Source: Walker, H. M. (1998). First steps to prevent antisocial behavior. *Teaching Exceptional Children 30*(4), 16–19.

Methods and Strategies 5.6 looks at ways to gain an understanding of learners' unique needs.

Methods and Strategies 5.6:
Understanding Learners' Unique Needs

To determine the specific (and the extent of) at-risk conditions or behaviors for management purposes, teachers can:

1. Collaborate with other professionals (e.g., counselors and special education personnel) as well as parents and families.
2. Use appropriate diagnostic tests and checklists of learner characteristics.
3. Check learners' permanent records as well as previous teachers.
4. Talk with learners to determine their perceptions of problems and possible efforts to address their individual needs.

Second, teachers need to respond appropriately to problem behavior. For example, teachers need to direct their attention to appropriate instruction and skill development rather than more control. They need to implement a wide variety of methods to help problem students learn new behavior skills and coping mechanisms (Jones & Jones, 1990). Some management methods used with other students might also be appropriate for learners at-risk; however, the most effective teachers seek to understand the causes of the misbehavior prior to making definitive conclusions about problem behavior and how to correct it.

Third, as discussed in chapter 2 and chapter 6, teachers need to involve parents and community in the implementation of at-risk programs. Some learners at-risk come from home settings that seriously affect their ability to function in school. In these cases, it is important that individuals skilled in community assistance be available to provide parental support (Jones & Jones, 1990).

Methods and Strategies 5.7 looks at ways to involve parents, family, and the community. Readers are reminded that Chapter 6 focuses entirely on involving parents and families.

Methods and Strategies 5.7:
Involving Parents, Family, and the Community.

1. Help parents and other family members understand how children being at-risk might affect classroom behaviors and management.
2. Ask parents and other family members for their opinions of at-risk conditions and behaviors as well as their advice on appropriate intervention.
3. Ask parents to visit and assume active participatory roles in their child's educative and behavior-management efforts.
4. Help parents accept their child's limitations as well as strengths and efforts.
5. Ask parents to participate in evaluative and assessment efforts and in the planning and implementation of educational programs.

Fourth, teachers of learners at-risk sometimes received their professional training in other areas of education. Also, most teacher education programs offer only a course or two in the areas dealing with learners at-risk, usually an introductory course and possibly a methods course. However, teachers need to develop the professional expertise to work with learners at-risk. The professional expertise includes competencies and skills in characteristics of learners at-risk, methods and strategies, classroom environment, management and organization, and parent and family participation, just to name a few.

Fifth, a teacher might ask, "How can I gain such competencies and skills?" We think teachers can work toward effective management skills by taking college coursework, participating in workshops, collaborating with other teachers, and reading professional journals and books.

Table 5.2 looks at several questions teachers might ask as they evaluate management effectiveness.

Table 5.2—Evaluating Management Effectiveness

1. Do management efforts include an understanding of the unique needs of learners at-risk? Do management efforts reflect an appropriate response (e.g., fair and equitable) to problem behavior?

2. Does the classroom management contribute to learners at-risk feeling physically and psychologically safe? Do they feel safe dealing with teachers and other students, both within the classroom and other areas of the school?

3. Do management efforts reflect an understanding of learners' development (such as young childhood, middle childhood, or later childhood)?

4. Are learners provided with clear and abbreviated classroom rules? Do they feel responsible for their own behavior? Do fewer rules exist rather than more?

5. Do learners feel a sense of community? Do they feel they are treated as individuals and with a sense of fairness and justice? Do they feel a sense of collaboration in the educational process?

6. Are learners' shorter attention spans reflected in all aspects of the management program? Are students allowed to move around the classroom in worthwhile educational pursuits?

7. Are learners' socialization needs addressed? Are programs in place to teach appropriate socialization skills? Do conflict management skills teach students appropriate ways to avoid violent confrontations?

8. Do management efforts recognize the needs of and help specific special needs learners? Are management efforts clearly stated in the Individualized Educational Program (IEP) when one is required?

9. Does the management program involve parents, families, and community members? Do learners perceive their parents are involved in and support teachers' management efforts?

10. Do management efforts suggest teachers have the appropriate skills and competencies to work with students at-risk?

Developed from: LeBoeuf, D., & Delany-Shabazz, R. V. (1997, March). Conflict resolution. *Office of Juvenile Justice and Delinquency Prevention* (Fact Sheet #55). Washington, DC: U. S. Department of Justice.

Last, teachers can provide conflict resolution that allows students to work through conflicts in socially acceptable ways. Conflict resolution programs can teach K–8 learners how to manage conflict and reduce violence, confrontations, suspensions, and disciplinary referrals. Conflict resolution teaches learners how to express their views and seek mutually acceptable solutions. The most effective programs involve the school community, are integrated into the educational curriculum, and are linked to family and community mediation initiatives (LeBoeuf & Delany-Shabazz, 1997). Table 5.3 summarizes four general approaches to conflict resolution.

Table 5.3—Four Approaches to Conflict Resolution

Process Curriculum
Educators teach the principles and processes of conflict resolution as distinct lessons such as the *Program for Young Negotiators* which provides for learners and educators practicing principled negotiation as a means of dispute resolution. Another program, *Fighting Fair* in North Carolina, uses a process curriculum (as an integral part of the curriculum) and has experienced promising results such as impressive reductions in school, as well as out-of-school, suspensions.

Peer Mediation
Educators teach learners to counsel and work with children to find resolutions to conflicts. In Las Vegas, NV, the schools and social services provide a comprehensive school-based mediation program in several elementary and middle schools. Results include peer mediators successfully resolving 86 percent of the conflicts they mediated, and fewer physical fights occurred on the school grounds

> **Peaceable Classroom**
> Educators provide a whole-class methodology that includes teaching students the abilities, principles, and problem-solving processes of conflict resolution.
>
> **Peaceable School**
> Educators build on the peaceable classroom by integrating conflict resolution into the management of the school with every person working in the school having training in conflict resolution.
>
> Developed from: LeBoeuf, D., & Delany-Shabazz, R. V. (1997, March). Conflict resolution. *Office of Juvenile Justice and Delinquency Prevention* (Fact Sheet #55). Washington, DC: U. S. Department of Justice.

Teachers' Management Styles and Procedures

As we stated earlier, we see management as including both students *and* teachers. Most educators understand what is meant by "student behavior," but some have a less developed idea of "teacher behavior." We firmly believe that teachers' behaviors have significant effects on student behavior. The teachers' perspectives on actual management procedures affect daily mindsets toward learners at-risk and actual management decisions. Likewise, we think teaching behaviors affect student behaviors. The teacher who is well-planned, organized, an effective manager, and capable of smooth transitions from one learning activity to another often have well-behaved students. Exceptions, of course, exist, but the contrary also holds true—teachers with less capable management skills often experience more student misbehaviors.

Teachers' Management Styles

As with most educational endeavors, classroom management can take more than one direction. Some teachers seek to manage cooperatively because they believe students participate more harmoniously when they have input into management decisions. Teachers give students an opportunity to talk about advantages and disadvantages of various educational arrangements and the means to test promising possibilities. In these classrooms, decision making is a cooperative enterprise, revealing a respect for both individual and group welfare. The teacher's democratic management style invites involvement, creates a sense of community, and works toward practices that reflect reasoned choices and commonly held expectations.

Other teachers have a different management style. They establish standards and insist on strict obedience. They believe that cooperation results because the teacher offers a convincing rationale for the decisions that affect students' well-being. He or she expects students to abide by the established classroom rules. This more authoritarian management style presumes that sound judgement and just decisions can be rendered without collaboration (Froyen, 1988).

It will probably not come as a surprise that we believe learners at-risk will be more likely to cooperate and give their best, both behaviorally and academically, when teachers invite harmony, allow them to suggest rules, and encourage them to work cooperatively. While some learners at-risk feel disenfranchised and alienated; they might be unaccustomed to having their views and opinions sought. It is very likely that they will respond favorably when teachers invite their cooperation and ask for their opinions of the classroom management system.

Teachers' Management Procedures

Teachers we know often equate teaching behaviors with management behaviors, i.e., teachers who use effective teaching techniques are usually effective managers. Selected examples of effective teaching behaviors that contribute to positive classroom management include using workable and efficient instructional methods and strategies, emphasizing productive time on task (rather than just "busy" work), keeping students informed of intended objectives, and harboring success expectations—both for academics and behavior.

Technique 1—"Withitness"—Workable and Efficient. Jacob Kounin (1970) and Jere Brophy (1983) suggested that teachers should demonstrate "withitness"—the teacher knows all learners' behaviors and knows without hesitation whether behaviors contribute to or take away from effective management. Effective managers demonstrate specific "withit" behaviors such as eliminating or lessening problems before they become disruptive, monitoring all classroom activities, and positioning themselves where all students can be seen at all times. Students realize their teacher knows all behaviors and detects inappropriate behaviors early and accurately. For example, while helping an individual student during seatwork, a teacher monitors other students, acknowledges other requests for assistance, handles disruptions, and keeps track of time. During a discussion, a teacher listens to student answers, watches other students for signs of comprehension or confusion, thinks of the next question, and scans the class for possible misbehaviors. At the same time, the teacher attends to the pace of the discussion, the sequence of selecting students to answer, the relevance and quality of answers, and the logical development of content (Doyle, 1986).

Technique 2—"Productive Time" on Task. Herbert Walberg (1988) proposed "productive time" to be time spent on lessons rather than just engaged time, i.e., tasks designed to keep learners busy and quiet. Walberg proposed that only a fraction of engaged time proves productive since conventional "whole-group" instruction cannot accommodate the vast differences in individual learning rates and prior knowledge. In other words, teachers can contribute to classroom management by engaging learners in appropriate work that matches individual learner's abilities and interests. Specifically, teachers can provide:

1. Appropriately-paced learning activities rather than expecting learners to learn a great deal of information in a short time, thus reducing students' frustration levels and perceived need to behave.

2. Learning goals and instructional activities accurately reflecting learners' at-risk conditions or behaviors, prior achievement, age or stage of maturation, motivational levels, and self-esteem which can lessen learners' need to misbehave for recognition.

3. School environments which reflect an appreciation for time being efficiently and effectively used, thus reducing learners' needs to engage in undesirable behaviors. Instructional activities are age-, ability-, and developmentally-appropriate and contribute to useful and relevant learning objectives.

Technique 3—Keeping Students Informed of Intended Objectives. Research by Porter and Brophy (1988) stressed the importance of teachers being clear about learning goals and providing learners with strategies to enhance learning. Effective teachers know content and instructional strategies, make expert use of instructional materials, demonstrate an understanding of students, and address specific objectives. Teachers should be clear about goals to prevent learner confusion, communicate to students expectations for both learning and behavior, monitor students' learning progress to determine areas of frustration, teach students the metacognitive strategies needed for efficient and effective learning, and reflect on their instructional and management practices (Porter & Brophy 1988).

Technique 4—Success Expectations—Both for Academics and Behavior. Thomas Good and Jere Brophy (1994) suggest learners need to set realistic success expectations and develop a commitment to work toward those expectations. For example, learners who set goals of moderate difficulty (neither too hard nor too easy) exert more effort and persistence, offer a serious commitment to pursuing goals rather than considering them as mere hopes, and concentrate on achieving success rather than avoiding failure.

Unfortunately, some learners, especially learners at-risk, have lost faith in their ability to learn and to achieve academically. Motivating learners should include convincing them to believe in their teacher and themselves. Teachers, realizing the powerful effects of motivation, convey the possibility of accomplishing learning goals increases when learners establish goals and work diligently and determinedly toward goals.

Learners might misbehave because they feel unable to succeed at academic tasks. Some learners who establish unrealistic goals (or whose teachers set unrealistically high goals) might think academic pursuits only result in failure.

Therefore, misbehaving seems easier than putting forth effort toward achiev-ing learning goals. Teachers can help students select realistic short-term and long-term goals and help students acquire proper study habits, maintain an as-signment guide, take books home, and study for tests.

Methods and Strategies 5.8 suggests teaching behaviors which contribute to classroom management.

 ## Methods and Strategies 5.8: Teaching Behaviors that Contribute to Classroom Management

1. Knowing students' strengths, weaknesses, and learning needs enables teachers to better address individual learning needs, thus reducing rea-sons for misbehavior.

2. Being clear about instructional goals and activities and communicat-ing clear expectations to students—and why—leave little reason for students to be off-task due to confusion about teacher expectations.

3. Monitoring students' understanding by offering regular and appropri-ate feedback contributes to students realizing the teacher knows their actions and progress and reduces the likelihood that they will engage in inappropriate behaviors.

4. Making expert use of curricular materials and instructional methods reduces the chance of students demonstrating off-task behaviors.

5. Teaching students metacognitive strategies and providing actual op-portunities contribute to students' feeling successful with school expe-riences (Porter & Brophy 1988).

Summary

Learners at-risk deserve a classroom environment and organization that contribute to their behavior as well as their academic achievement. Rather than mandating more rules for learners at-risk, some educators have found that fewer rules and more freedom result in students accepting greater responsibility for their behavior. Such a management style requires that teachers encourage co-operation. Lest it appear that this "cooperative" management style means lower expectations for behavior and achievement, it is quite the contrary. Implement-ing a cooperative management style continues to mean high expectations, a physically and psychologically safe classroom, and a safe and orderly environ-ment in which to learn. It has been our experience that this management style can become a reality, especially when teachers genuinely believe in coopera-tion and teach learners at-risk the value of working collaboratively toward posi-tive and humane goals.

Additional Information and Resources

Abrams, B. J., & Segal, A. (1998). How to prevent aggressive behavior. *Teaching Exceptional Children, 30*(4), 10–15. Abrams and Segal look at the dynamics of aggression, elements of positive classroom climate, and ways to teach alternative behavior.

Erb, T. (1997). Student-friendly classrooms in a not very child-friendly world. *Middle School Journal 28*(4), 2. In this insightful editorial comment, Erb maintains acknowledging and validating student needs can result in an orderly and humane learning environment.

Charles, C. M. (1999). *Building classroom discipline* (6th ed.). White Plains, NY: Longman. In this excellent book, C. M. Charles examines in considerable detail the major classroom management theories and offers examples of how each can be implemented.

Schmid, R. E. (1998). Three steps to self-discipline. *Teaching Exceptional Children, 30*(4), 36–39. Schmid explains three steps to self-discipline and describes the impact of the effort.

Sergiovanni, T. J. (1994). *Building community in schools*. San Francisco: Jossey-Bass. Sergiovanni looks at relationships in communities, emerging school communities, school curriculum, school communities, and building communities of learners.

The Rader School, http://rader-inc.com/overview.htm The mission of the Rader Schools is to create a quality, respectful learning environment that provides innovative programs to improve unacceptable behaviors.

Chapter 6	# Parents and Families

Overview

Although all children and educators benefit when parents and families participate and collaborate in school activities and the learning process, the need for involvement of parents and families of learners at-risk might be even more crucial in the overall educational process. Learners' achievement can increase; at-risk conditions and behaviors can decrease; and parents and families can better understand their child's at-risk characteristics as well as educator's efforts. With the goal of involving parents and nurturing parent-teacher-child relationships, teachers can work to engage parents through involvement activities, parent advisory councils, and parent conferences. Caring and creative teachers can undoubtedly think of other ways to strengthen the bond between parents and schools. The important key will be to remember that the parents of children at-risk might face special challenges, thus resulting in different involvement activities and conference strategies.

Chapter Objectives

After reading and thinking about this chapter on parents and families of learners at-risk, the reader should be able to:

1. Explain the crucial need for both parents and families participating and collaborating with teachers in the overall educational process of learners at-risk.

2. Explain how parents and families of learners at-risk can play a number of vital roles—roles that educators need to encourage and strengthen.

3. Define parent and family involvement, offer several reasons for parent involvement in education, and describe the characteristics of effective parent involvement programs.

4. Suggest several barriers to parent and family involvement and several keys to overcoming these barriers.

5. Explain the purposes of parent advisory councils and how they can be used to involve and seek the opinions of parents.

6. Explore parent conferences and several suggestions for making meetings with parents more effective and productive.

The Need for Involving Parents and Families of Learners At-Risk

A positive relationship between home and school has the potential for resulting in improved achievement and behavior as well as more positive interpersonal relationships. In fact, both parents and educators benefit when educators exert the time and effort to build a positive working relationship—one that allows and, in fact, promotes a collaborative effort to help the learner at-risk. Also, both parents and educators can gain a clearer understanding of at-risk conditions and behaviors, i.e., whether an at-risk condition or behavior actually exists, the nature of the problem, the evidence of the problem at home, and the intervention needed to address the condition or behavior. Opinions and comments offered by both immediate parents and extended family members can be valuable identification indicators (i.e., type, severity, and possible intervention plan) of at-risk conditions and behaviors, thus complementing the identification devices described in chapter 1.

Methods and Strategies 6.1 looks at ways to determine parent and family needs.

Methods and Strategies 6.1: Determining Parent and Family Needs

Develop a survey to determine needs that parents and families of children at-risk consider important. While the survey should reflect the individual community, possible survey items include living with children at-risk, dealing with teachers and administrators, and seeking help from referral agencies. Instead of having only "yes" and "no" questions, include open-ended questions such as "What do you want discussed in a parent education session?" or "What special needs do parents and families of children at-risk have?

Parents and Families of Learners At-Risk

Parents and families of learners at-risk can play a number of vital roles—roles that educators need to encourage and enhance. Naturally, some parents may be more astute in helping their children than others; however, all parents can help learners at-risk to some degree. Educators have a responsibility to help parents to a point where they can be assets in the education process. Such a responsibility includes teaching parents about ways to help their child as well as about the condition or behavior that places the child at-risk.

Strengthening Parents' Roles

Effective teachers of learners at-risk provide parents with meaningful in-volvement activities. As will be discussed in more detail later, teachers encourage parents to get involved in programs that reflect the needs of learners at-risk and assist children with their particular at-risk condition or behavior. We have found effective parent involvement consists of more than just "helping" the teacher such as filing papers, duplicating handouts, grading papers, and recording grades. The effort we suggest includes actual teaching individuals and small groups, participating on advisory councils focusing on educating children at-risk, and parent-teacher-counselor committees that decide actual intervention procedures. Parents need to feel their efforts are influential, and children need to know of their parents' involvement. One planning committee on which we served in an elementary school always had three parents. The committee met on a regular basis and when the parents were unable to attend, the chair rescheduled the meeting. Rather than giving only lip service to parent involvement, this school demonstrated its commitment to seeking parental input.

Some schools organize parent support groups, so parents can get to know one another and benefit from others' experiences. Parents of children at-risk sometimes feel they are different—their children's needs as well as their parental needs. One school has a parent support group that meets twice a month for two hours. Activities include guest speakers, small group discussions, unplanned discussions between parents before and after the meeting, and times for parents to suggest how the school can better meet their needs and their children's needs. Teacher representatives from the various grades attend the parent support group to offer advice and counsel. Rather than taking a generic approach, topics focus on an array of at-risk needs, conditions, and behaviors. One parent we know stated, "It gives us a chance to see we are not the only ones facing a particular problem. Others are in the same boat—facing the same or very similar problems. Also, we are in some ways fortunate—our situations could be worse, and in some ways, we are indeed lucky."

Some schools also use a team approach to provide guidance and counseling to parents. Parents often either cannot afford or do not know guidance professionals outside the school. Either individual, group, or family, these guidance services focus on how parents and families can deal with children and their various at-risk conditions. The guidance professionals work closely with the teachers to learn specific problems to address as well as to learn the teachers' efforts. Sometimes, guidance counselors perceive the problems are too acute or outside their professional domain, and therefore, suggest private counseling agencies or social service agencies. This guidance approach recognizes that at-risk conditions and behaviors affect immediate and extended family members as well as the individual child. The teacher is often the first to recognize the need for guidance services and makes the initial suggestion to the parent as well as the initial contact with the guidance professional.

Methods and Strategies 6.2 looks at how educators can provide guidance support.

Methods and Strategies 6.2:
Providing Guidance Support

Arrange for several guidance and counseling professionals and other qualified educators to have about four concurrent sessions during which parents can learn about a number of topics such as parenting children at-risk, challenges with socialization, parental rights and responsibilities, and specific at-risk conditions and behaviors, and other identified parental concerns.

Parent education workshops and other educational opportunities are other ways in which teachers can assist parents with children at-risk, enhance knowledge of family life, teach techniques for changing attitudes and behaviors, help parents change their own negative behaviors, and teach parents how to help in the education of their child. It has been our experience in designing such programs that parents become more involved and develop more positive attitudes toward school activities. Workshops can focus on a number of challenges related to learners at-risk: describing specific at-risk conditions and behaviors; telling about ways parents can help learners at-risk; describing how parents can be an integral part of a collaborative team; and helping parents identify additional referral sources. Such parent education programs or workshops, of course, should be based on specific at-risk conditions and behaviors as well as specific parental needs and concerns.

Research and Classroom Practice 6.1 describes a parent education program on violence intervention.

Research and Classroom Practice 6.1:
Preventing School Violence

These authors described Padres Trabajando por la Paz (PTP), a violence intervention program for Hispanic parents to increase parental monitoring of student behavior. This parent education intervention program is designed to prevent school violence such as homicide, assault, delinquency, and victimization.

The PTP program provides an explicit, step-by-step guide to integrating theory, empirical findings from the literature, and data collected from parents and families in the development of a parent education program. The process includes intervention, needs assessment, and program evaluation.

The five steps include: Step 1—designing program objectives that address the parents and their children. Step 2—matching intervention models from theory, literature, and information collected from the parents. Step 3—translating methods into practical strategies. Step 4—program adoption and strategies. Step 5—planning for monitoring and evaluation.

Implications for classroom practice include:

1. Ask children about their plans when they leave the house such as where they are going, who they will be with, and when they plan to return.

2. Obtain a list of telephone numbers of children's friends, so contact, if necessary, can be made.

3. Call parents of the child's friends to show concern and interest and to make parental expectations known.

4. Visit the school to participate in parent education programs and to learn of efforts to reduce violence.

Source: Murray, N., Kelder, S., Parcel, G., & Orphinas, P. (1998). Development of an intervention map for a parent education intervention to prevent violence among Hispanic middle school students. *Journal of School Health, 68*(2), 46–52.

Methods and Strategies 6.3 offers several "considerations" when planning parent workshops.

Methods and Strategies 6.3: Planning Parent Workshops

Make a list of "planning considerations" for parent workshops, i.e., being familiar with all workshop materials and activities, preparing name tags, arranging the room for the meeting, and preparing signs indicating where to meet. Plan to involve parents in the meeting, but do not ask parents to speak unless they volunteer. Consider your audience—be careful to avoid educational jargon and terms that parents might not understand. Other planning considerations undoubtedly can be listed.

Parent and Family Involvement

Defining the Issue

The positive effects of parent involvement on student achievement and overall school progress suggest a need to involve parents in the education of learners at-risk. The issue, however, is more complex than simply convincing parents to visit the school. It includes conscientious efforts in several areas: explaining the school's efforts to help learners at-risk, making parents feel welcome and valued in their child's education, educating parents about their children and their at-risk conditions and behaviors, and involving parents in their children's education whenever possible.

Reasons for Parent Involvement in Education

The reasons for, and advantages of, parents and teachers working as partners and for teachers providing appropriate educational experiences for parents have been well documented. There is a strong positive relationship between parent involvement and school achievement, increased student attendance, positive parent-child communication, improved student attitudes and behavior, and more parent-community support of the schools (Chavkin, 1989). Although children of all backgrounds are unique and deserve the full consideration of teachers and parents, parents of children at-risk might be in even greater need. There is much to be gained, in terms of improved overall school achievement and improved cultural and interpersonal relationships between parents, teachers, and students, when educators accept the challenge of working with parents in the hope of helping children at-risk.

Characteristics of Effective Parent Involvement Programs

The Southwest Educational Development Laboratory (SEDL) identified and described characteristics of promising parent involvement programs. Table 6.1 shows seven characteristics of effective parent involvement programs.

Table 6.1—Seven Characteristics of Effective Parent Involvement Programs

1. Written policies legitimize the importance of parent involvement and help frame the program context.

2. Administrative support includes a budget for implementing programs, material and product resources, and people with designated responsibilities.

3. Training programs are in place for both educators and parents.

4. Programs emphasize partnership and collaborative approaches.

5. Two-way communication between the home and the school occurs frequently and on a regular basis.

6. Networking identifies additional resources and encourages people to share information, resources, and technique expertise.

7. Regular evaluation, during key stages and at the end of the cycle or phase of the program, provides indicators of progress and outcomes.

Developed from: Williams, D. L., & Chavkin, N. F. (1989). Essential elements of strong parent involvement programs. *Educational Leadership, 47*(2), 18–20.

While the characteristics listed in table 6.1 do not specifically reflect programs for learners at-risk, they have implications for teachers wanting to involve parents of learners at-risk. For example, effective parent involvement programs usually have written policies (prepared collaboratively by parents, teachers, and administrators) that reflect the purpose of the at-risk program. Also, administrators voice their support and provide training for both teachers and parents. Using a partnership approach, teachers design and implement two-way communication designed especially for parents of learners at-risk. As with most effective programs, regular evaluation occurs and is followed up with action to remedy weaknesses.

Ten Factors Essential to School-Home Collaboration

Barbara Jackson and Bruce Cooper (1993) wrote about factors essential to effective school-home collaboration. While their article focused mainly on urban high schools, their factors also apply to elementary and middle schools.

1. *Leadership*—Principals provide effective and active leadership, both to other school personnel as well as parents.
2. *Accessibility*—Open lines of communication between parents and educators increase the chances of successful collaboration.
3. *Time*—Educators have sufficient time to plan, recruit, and follow up with parents.
4. *Cultural awareness*—Educators understand the culture of the parents and communities, which leads to increased trust.
5. *Active teacher roles*—Teachers are actively involved with parents in all aspects of the program.
6. *Continuity*—Continuous and regular attendance in group meetings allows all members to build a sense of community and ownership.
7. *Public recognition*—Parents and other participants function in a visible manner which is essential to building confidence and continued support.
8. *Broad-based support*—Involvement of outside community groups to assist and help sell the school to the larger community.
9. *Adolescent focus*—Again, this article focused on high schools, so in this case, elementary schools and middle schools need to have a program that focuses on developmentally appropriate practice.
10. *Recognition of parents as people*—There needs to be a recognition of the needs and interests of parents as people who are interested in the success of their children as well as the involvement program (Jackson & Cooper, 1993).

Methods and Strategies 6.4 looks at what needs to be included when planning specially designed programs.

Methods and Strategies 6.4: Planning Specially Designed Programs

Outline what you might need to include in a program designed to address specific at-risk conditions and behaviors, i.e., a program for low achievers, unmotivated learners, or drug/alcohol users. Pinpoint characteristics that programs should reflect in order to address specific children at-risk rather than a general approach that attempts to address general at-risk conditions and behaviors.

Recommendations

Our experience designing and implementing parent involvement programs for learners at-risk allows us to offer several recommendations:

1. *Educate parents about at-risk conditions and behaviors.* Many parents feel overwhelmed or bewildered and do not understand what their child is experiencing. Thus, they often blame the child or blame themselves for the at-risk condition or behavior. One parent asked us, "Was this caused by something I did? After her father and I separated, she started having these problems. I really blame myself for all this." We told her that the parents separating might have affected the young girl, but it was unlikely that this particular problem was caused by the family change. Teachers can play helpful roles and demonstrate caring attitudes as they teach parents about the challenges facing their children.

Also, teachers should convey the feeling that their child being at-risk does not mean "all hope is lost"—ways exist to address at-risk conditions and behaviors. Teachers can explain efforts to address at-risk conditions and behaviors—describing school programs and their purposes, providing assistance with individual children, and helping parents to see children's progress.

2. *Offer parents meaningful roles in the educational experiences of their child at-risk.* Parents should be offered opportunities to help *their* child. This includes actually conducting tutoring sessions, participating in advisement sessions, and helping with the selection of instructional materials. Such a recommendation also includes offering families opportunities to support learning such as serving on advisory councils, participating in parent-teacher conferences, and serving as parent representatives on collaborative teams. Innovative and thoughtful teachers can undoubtedly think of other ways to provide parents with roles that they will consider genuinely beneficial.

3. *Keep parents informed about children's at-risk conditions and behaviors—the nature and severity as well as teacher and child progress.* We overheard Mrs. Dyar say "We really know little about what is going on at school. We get reports cards, of course, but other than that, we are pretty much kept in the dark." Most teachers will agree that this is not how parents should feel. Parents should be kept well informed about at-risk conditions and behavior as well as progress toward overcoming them. Teachers can keep parents informed through telephone calls, home visits, e-mail, written reports, parent conferences, and any other way that conveys information. Parents should never wonder about children's progress—they should always feel informed, welcome to visit the classroom during stated visitation times, and feel comfortable asking to see their child's records. It has been our experience that parents who feel informed about their child's progress will be more willing to assist in the educative effort and to support the overall school program.

Case Study 6.1 explains how the teachers at Four Oaks Elementary School planned and implemented a parent involvement program.

Case Study 6.1: The Four Oaks
Parent Involvement Program

Four Oaks Elementary School had four teachers who worked exclusively with students at-risk. At a meeting with two consultants, they shared their concerns over the lack of parent involvement in their efforts to help learners at-risk. Some of the items mentioned included parents rarely visited the school, did not offer their services, and showed little or no understanding of the need for their participation in their children's education.

The teachers briefly listed possible reasons for the lack of involvement such as parents did not care, did not know how to be involved, felt threatened by educators, and perhaps felt embarrassed about their children being at-risk. They agreed that while the reasons were important, it was even more important to think of ways to get parents to participate—they needed a plan, with specific goals, activities, and a timetable. Some voiced skepticism that the plan would work. One teacher stated, "Parents at this school have never been involved; it is doubtful whether any of this will work. Let's face it—we might be setting ourselves up to fail."

Planned activities included scheduling conferences with the hope parents would attend, planning parent involvement activities, offering parenting workshops, and encouraging parents to work on committees. They agreed they first had to get parents' attention: efforts included sending notices home with students, requesting free television and radio advertising time, asking social service agencies to encourage parents, and posting notices in churches and synagogues. Second, they needed to make the school "parent friendly." All key school personnel would attend an information session such as a "customer-relations" training session for the purpose of making parents feel welcome at school. Third, the group decided to continue planning the remainder of the year and begin actual implementation the next year.

For the parent intervention to be successful, the teachers knew they needed an assessment system. Such a system included more than just a tabulation of "numbers." They wanted to look at the "quality" of the participation, such as reasons for visits or involvement and whether beneficial outcomes resulted. Possible evaluative questions might be, "Why did the parents come to school?" "to help or to complain?" "to learn?" "to participate in groups?" They agreed to meet at the middle and end of each semester to discuss programs and reassess their plan.

Methods and Strategies 6.5 calls for educators to suggest ways to provide opportunities to support learning.

Methods and Strategies 6.5:
Providing Opportunities to Support Learning

Make a list of ways that parents and families can support learning for children at-risk. This sheet could be distributed at parent involvement sessions or parent conferences. While the list will depend upon the specific at-risk conditions and behaviors, examples might include helping with homework, attending family counseling sessions, taking children to libraries and other educational sites, attending parent conferences, and being sure reading materials are available at home. Think of as many opportunities as you can that will provide parents with opportunities to help their child.

Promoting the Success of Parent Involvement Programs
Sandra Schurr (1993) maintained that parents and educators are victims of outdated perceptions that result in barriers to parent participation in schools. For example, educators can no longer rely on stereotypical views of family needs and how these needs can be addressed. Also, some parents of today's students might still recall their own school experiences, often with tyrannical teachers whose goals were to keep parents and children in line. Proven strategies offered by Schurr (1993) for involving parents included:

1. Mutual goal settings, contracting, and evaluating.
2. Assessment of school policies, practices, and rituals.
3. Establishment of a parent lounge/center/resource room.
4. Public information displays, public service messages, and work-site seminars.
5. Parent handbook of guidelines and tips.
6. Weekend or evening public information fair.
7. Parent and student exchange day, whereby parents follow students' routines for a day.
8. Extra academic credit for students for parent involvement.
9. Schoolwide communication plan.
10. Parent/teacher dialogue journals for clearer communication.
11. Home visits for a special bond.
12. Schoolwide homework policy.

Barriers to Parent and Family Involvement

Barriers
K–8 teachers usually realize the number of barriers that hinder parent and family involvement. Potential barriers include language difficulties, lack of parental teaching skills, limited financial resources, lack of transportation and childcare, employment schedules, feelings of alienation, feeling unable to cope

with children, feeling intimidated by school officials, and feeling unwelcome at school (Loucks & Waggoner, 1999). While Loucks and Waggoner (1999) referred primarily to the overall school population, barriers for parents of learners at-risk might be more acute. As teachers work toward increasing parental involvement, they need to understand the added difficulties many families of learners at-risk face. For example, parents might feel embarrassed due to their children being at-risk or they might feel overwhelmed at having to deal with the extra responsibilities. They might misunderstand programs and efforts, might not understand their responsibilities, and might resent their attendance at meetings. Also, they feel might "guilty" that they have contributed to the at-risk conditions or behaviors in some way.

Keys to Overcoming Barriers

Table 6.2 looks at a number of keys to overcoming barriers to parent and family involvement.

Table 6.2—Keys to Overcoming Barriers to Parent and Family Involvement

1. Translate materials into parents' native language, if the parents speak a native language other than English.
2. Provide activities that can be done at home that require little training and parent education.
3. Distribute information about community service organizations and make appropriate social services referrals.
4. Provide transportation and child care.
5. Schedule breakfast or evening meetings or arrange to meet at a place of employment.
6. Ask other families to help make contact and involve community leaders.
7. Offer parent and family workshops and discussion groups to give adults a forum to express their concerns while seeking advice from them.
8. Make personal contacts—call home, do a home visit, send an e-mail, or write a note.
9. Focus on positive attributes and provide positive examples of work.
10. Make parents and families feel welcome at school by providing training to office staff, offering parents a tour, and providing information about the school.

Source: Loucks, H. E., & Waggoner, J. E. (1999, Spring). Outreach to families. *Classroom Connections*, 1(4), 1.

Methods and Strategies 6.6 asks teachers to propose ways to determine and overcome barriers.

Methods and Strategies 6.6:
Determining and Overcoming Barriers

In table 6.2, we have listed several barriers that might impede parental involvement. Consider your own school and children at-risk to determine other barriers that might be specific to a given situation. List the barriers on the left and the possible solutions on the right.

Reaching Disengaged Parents

Educators reaching out to parents often experience frustration that their efforts do not extend to parents who most need assistance. Catherine Petersen and Ellen Warnsby (1993) described Project Better Day, an effort to identify 25 uninvolved parents of children in grades 1–4, to draw them into a positive relationship with the school, and provide them with training to help them help their children succeed in school. First, Petersen and Warnsby (1993) explained that hard-to-reach parents are often preoccupied with personal difficulties such as being on welfare, living at survival rates, and being unprepared to meet the demands of society. They often had negative experiences with school during childhood and continue to hold resentments which might influence the attitudes and values of their children. Furthermore, these parents might be struggling with other aspects of adult life leaving them with negative perceptions of their self-worth, feelings of alienation from the larger society and school, and insecurity associated with school personnel.

Project Better Day encouraged schools to use community agencies—churches, neighborhood centers, and boys and girls clubs as buffers between the school and parents. Next, the schools invited the parents to nonthreatening gatherings that included their children. The schools then planned a series of contacts with the parents that progressed from bolstering the parents' self-worth to helping them with parenting skills. The project's major components included an outreach committee to conduct the project, an action plan to assess parent involvement and develop new recruitment methods, parent leadership training to develop commitment and leadership skills, gatherings of hard-to-reach parents to establish trust, and a Reading at Home course (Petersen & Warnsby, 1993).

Advisory Councils

A parent advisory council can be an excellent means of providing parents and families of children at-risk with opportunities to voice opinions and generally influence the overall operation of the school. By having an effective parent advisory council, council representatives (or parents who make suggestions and comments through selected representatives) can offer specific suggestions on devising the school curriculum and making the teaching and learning environment more conducive to learners at-risk. Although we cannot provide a detailed list of topics, council members might want to discuss the purposes and goals of the program, procedures for being admitted to the at-risk program, ways to keep in contact with parents, methods and strategies used in the program, policies and regulations, community involvement, effects of the curriculum and instructional processes on learners at-risk, and cases involving individual students (provided the advisory council is privy to such information).

Methods and Strategies 6.7 asks readers to suggest ways to get parents involved in advisory roles.

Methods and Strategies 6.7: Getting Parents Involved in Advisory Roles

Propose several aspects that deserve considerations as teachers invite or encourage parents to participate in advisory councils, i.e., dealing with parents' reluctance, addressing confidentiality issues, showing appreciation for parents' participation, and making parents feel welcome and feel like integral contributing members. These are only representative examples—what other aspects deserve consideration?

Parent Conferences

Parent conferences can be a helpful mechanism for educating and involving parents as well as seeking their advice. While most parent conferences in which we have engaged have been positive, we admit to one or two that could have been improved. With effective planning, parent conferences usually benefit teachers and parents as well as children. This section offers some suggestions and tips for effective parent conferences.

The parent conference presents an opportunity for parents and teachers to exchange information about the child's school and home activities (i.e., activities that might contribute to the child being at-risk) and provides an occasion to involve parents in planning and implementing their child's at-risk program. Parents should always be told upfront about the purposes of the conference, especially when the teacher calls the conference. Teachers providing a written agenda might also lessen the parent's anxiety about the conference (Shea & Bauer, 1985).

Suggestions for Effective Parent Conferences

Spaulding (1994) offered four suggestions for effective parent conferences. These might be even more important for educators meeting with parents and families of learners at-risk.

1. Begin to work toward positive relationships with parents and families before school begins.
2. Talk regularly with students' parents; tell them of accomplishments and concerns, and ask for their advice and suggestions. Extra efforts

might be necessary to convince parents to become active participants.

3.   Ask students to join in parent conferences and to offer their opinions.

4.   Make the conference as comfortable as possible; reinforce students' accomplishments, avoid using confusing jargon, show parents how they can help, and end the conference on a positive note.

Other suggestions include: 1) maintain a positive tone and try to end the conference by reiterating positive points; 2) be truthful yet tactful, understanding parents of children at-risk might already have considerable apprehension; 3) respect parents and children's information as confidential; 4) observe professional ethics at all times; 5) listen to parents' comments, concerns, and suggestions; 6) invite parents to visit and participate in school activities; and 7) offer multiple solutions to at-risk conditions and behaviors.

Methods and Strategies 6.8 looks at ways to get parental comments and suggestions during conferences.

 ## Methods and Strategies 6.8: Getting Parental Comments and Suggestions During Conferences

Suggest how teachers can get parents of children at-risk to share comments and suggestions. Parents often feel uncomfortable or feel teachers are not interested in their opinions. Make a list of ways (perhaps consult a parent who feels comfortable or is vocal) teachers can show parents the importance of their comments and suggestions during parent conferences.

In table 6.3, we add several tips for effective conferences, all based upon our experiences with learners at-risk and their parents.

Table 6.3—Tips for Effective Conferences

1.   Explain the at-risk condition or behavior in terms that parents can understand—do not "talk down" to them, but be sure they understand the reason for their child being at-risk.

2.   Convince parents there is "hope"—do not let them leave the parent conference feeling despair or feel they have failed as parents.

3.   Explain the school's efforts and programs to help the child in multiple ways rather than just the specific at-risk condition or behavior.

4.   Offer information about referral services such as social service programs and community agencies that help children at-risk.

5.   Explain to parents the necessity of parent-teacher-child partnerships to help children at-risk—neither parents nor teachers should be expected to shoulder the entire responsibility. Plus, children need to see the coordinated efforts of parents and teachers working in their behalf.

Summary

Some teachers have told us that dealings, whether involvement or conferences, with parents of children at-risk can be more challenging than when working with parents of other children. One teacher said, "It is not difficult to tell a parent good news—the challenge comes with explaining how a child is at-risk." While this can be a little simplistic, we agree that dealing with parents of learners at-risk can be a little more challenging. Parents might feel guilty, might feel apprehensive, and might feel unable to cope. Still, teachers need to nurture the bond between parents and schools as well as provide direct assistance whenever possible. While teachers might need to sharpen their skills (e.g., learning about the needs of parents of children at-risk and learning how to offer appropriate involvement activities), we feel the results will be worth the effort for children, parents, and teachers.

Additional Information and Resources

Boveja, M. E. (1998). Parenting styles and adolescents' learning strategies in the urban community. *Journal of Multicultural Counseling and Development, 26*(2), 110–119. Boveja examines the relationship between parenting styles and urban adolescents' learning and studying strategies—while the article focuses primarily on adolescents, the implications also apply to younger children.

Lazar, A., & Slostad, F. (1999). How to overcome obstacles to parent-teacher partnerships. *The Clearing House, 72*(4), 206–219. These authors examine obstacles, call for systemic change, and suggest how parent-teacher partnerships can be more effective.

Koch, P. K., & McDonough, M. (1999). Improving parent-teacher conferences through collaborative conferences. *Young Children, 54*(2), 11–15. Koch and McDonough suggest a five-stage approach to making parent-teacher conferences more collaborative.

Parents and Teachers Talking Together, http:www.columbiagroup.org/parents.htm This organization is a structured dialogue that brings together adults who deal with Kentucky's children in an effort to improve education.

Improving the Achievement of At-Risk Students, http:www.minedu.govt.nz/Schools/Improving/Achievement/81.htm This resource provides provisions for monitoring and identifying student needs—one section focuses on "Fostering Relationships With Parents."

At-Risk Resources Buyers Guide, http:www.at-risk.com/prodv.htm. This resource provides parenting videos that focus on such topics as parenting difficult children and parenting special children. Other topics include sexuality, violence, and school success.

References

Abrams, B. J., & Segal, A. (1998). How to prevent aggressive behavior. *Teaching Exceptional Children, 30*(4), 10–15.

Alderman, M. K. (1990). Motivation for at-risk students. *Educational Leadership, 48*(1), 27–30.

Barth, R. P., Middleton, K., & Wagman, E. (1989). A skill building approach to preventing teenage pregnancy. *Theory into Practice, 28*(3), 183–190.

Bembry, J. X. (1998). Forming an educative community in the village. *Middle School Journal, 30*(1), 18–24.

Boveja, M. E. (1998). Parenting styles and adolescents' learning strategies in the urban community. *Journal of Multicultural Counseling and Development, 26*(2), 110–119.

Brophy, J. E. (1983). Classroom organization and management. *The Elementary School Journal, 83*(4), 265–285.

Burnet, D. (1999). Top ten points about being a continuous learner. http://www.thelearningcoach.com/10topcontinlearner.html

Canfield, J. (1990). Improving students' self-esteem. *Educational Leadership, 48*(1), 48–50.

Carbo, M. (1997). Learning style strategies that help at-risk students read and succeed. *Reaching Today's Youth: The Community Circle of Caring, 1*(2), 37–42

Carbo, M., & Hodges, H. (1988). Learning styles strategies can help students at risk. *Exceptional Children, 20*(4), 55–58.

Carnegie Council on Adolescent Development. (1989). *Turning points: Preparing American youth for the 21st century*. Washington, DC: Author.

Carroll, P. S., & Taylor, A. (1998). Understanding the culture of the classroom. *Middle School Journal, 30*(1), 9–17.

Charles, C. M. (1999). *Building classroom discipline* (6th ed.). White Plains, NY: Longman.

Chavkin, N. F. (1989). Debunking the myth about minority parents. *Educational Horizons, 67*(4), 119–123.

Clark, D. C., & Clark, S. N. (1998). Creating developmentally responsive learning environments. *Schools in the Middle, 8*(2), 12–15.

Come, B., & Fredericks, A. D. (1995). Family literacy in urban schools: Meeting the needs of at-risk children. *The Reading Teacher, 48*(7), 566–570.

Comer, J. (n.d.). A brief history and summary of the school development program. Unpublished manuscript, Yale University, Yale Child Study Center.

Conant, L. (1992). Characteristics of facilitative learning environments for students at-risk. ED 346421.

Cornett, C. E. (1983). *What should you know about teaching and learning styles.* Bloomington, IN: Phi Delta Kappa Education Foundation.

Crist, K. (1991). Restoring opportunity for dropouts. *Equity and Excellence in Education, 25*(1), 36–39.

Dana, T. M., & Collins, D. J. (1993). Considering alternative assessments for middle level learners. *Middle School Journal, 25*(2), 3–5.

Doyle, W. (1986). Classroom organization and management. In M. C. Wittock (Ed.), *Handbook of research on teaching* (3rd. ed), 392–431. New York: Macmillan.

Dunn, R. S., Dunn, K. J., & Price, G. E. (1986). *Learning style inventory manual.* Lawrence, KS: Price Systems.

Erb, T. (1997). Student-friendly classrooms in a not very child-friendly world. *Middle School Journal, 28*(4), 2.

Evertson, C. M., Emmer, E. T., Clements, B. S., & Worsham, M. E. (1994). *Classroom management for elementary teachers* (3rd. ed). Boston: Allyn and Bacon.

Finn, J. D. (1989). Withdrawing from school. *Review of Educational Research, 59,* 117–142.

Freiberg, H. J. (1998). Measuring school climate. *Educational Leadership, 56*(1), 22–26.

Froyen, L. A. (1988). *Classroom management: Empowering teacher-leaders.* Columbus, OH: Merrill.

Frymier, J., Barber, L., Carriedo, R., Denton, W., Gansneder, B., Johnson-Lewis, S., & Robertson, N. (1992). *Growing up is risky business, and schools are not to blame.* Final report, Phi Delta Kappa study of students at-risk, vol. 1. Bloomington, IN: Phi Delta Kappa.

Gable, R. A. (1994). *An ecological analysis of aggression: Implications for prevention and treatment.* Paper presented at the American Reeducation Association Conference, Nashville, TN.

Gan, S. L. (1999). Motivating at-risk students through computer-based cooperative learning activities. *Educational Horizons, 77*(3), 151–156.

Gardner, H. (1993). *Multiple intelligences: The theory in practice.* New York: Basic Books.

Ginott, H. (1971) *Teacher and child.* New York: Macmillan.

Good, T. L., & Brophy, J. E. (1994). *Looking in classrooms* (6th ed). New York: HarperCollins.

Graves, L. N. (1992). Cooperative learning communities: Context for a new vision of education and society. *Journal of Education, 174*, 57–79.

Griffith, J. (1998). The relation of school structure and social environment to parent involvement in elementary schools. *The Elementary School Journal, 99*(1), 53–80.

Groves, P. (1998). Meeting the needs of at-risk students: The day and night program. *The High School Journal, 81*(4), 251–257.

Gullatt, D. E., & Lofton, B. D. (1998). Helping at-risk learners succeed: A whole-school approach to success. *Schools in the Middle, 7*(4), 11–14, 42–43.

Hansen, J. M., & Childs, J. (1998). Creating a school where people like to be. *Educational Leadership, 56*(1), 14–17.

Harrison, J. A. (1998). A great LEAP forward. *The American School Board Journal, 185*(9), 44–45, 55.

Helge, D. (1990). *A national study regarding at-risk students (research report).* Bellingham, WA: National Rural Development Institute.

Hopfenberg, W. S., Lewin, H. M., Meister, G., & Rogers, J. (1991). *Accelerated schools.* Unpublished manuscript, Stanford University, Center for Educational Research at Stanford.

Hootstein, E. (1998). Motivating the unmotivated child. *Teaching K–8, 29*(3), 58–59.

Jackson, B. L., & Cooper, B. S. (1993). Involving parents in urban high schools. *The Education Digest, 58*(8), 27–31.

Jackson, B. R. (1999). Creating a climate of healing in a violent society. *Young Children, 52*(7), 68–70.

Jarolimek, J., & Foster, C. D. (1989). *Teaching and learning in the elementary school.* New York: Macmillan.

Jones, V. F., & Jones, L. S. (1990). *Comprehensive classroom management: Motivating and managing students* (3rd. ed). Boston: Allyn and Bacon.

Keefe, J. W., & Monk, J. S. (1986). *Learning style profile examiner's manual.* Reston, VA: NASSP.

Kellough, R. D., & Kellough, N. G. (1999). *Middle school teaching: A guide to methods and resources* (3rd ed.). Columbus, OH: Merrill/Prentice-Hall.

Koch, P. K., & McDonough, M. (1999). Improving parent-teacher conferences through collaborative conferences. *Young Children, 54*(2), 11–15.

Kostelnik, M. J., Rierdan, J., Whiren, A. P., & Soderman, A. K. (1998). *Guiding children's social development.* Cincinnati, OH: Brooks/Cole.

Kounin, J. S. (1970). *Discipline and group management in the classroom.* New York: Holt, Rinehart, and Winston.

Lange, C. M. (1998). Characteristics of alternative schools and programs serving at-risk students. *The High School Journal, 81*(4), 183–198.

Lazar, A., & Slostad, F. (1999). How to overcome obstacles to parent-teacher partnerships. *The Clearing House, 72*(4), 206–219.

LeBoeuf, D., & Delany-Shabazz, R. V. (1997, March). Conflict resolution. *Office of Juvenile Justice and Delinquency Prevention* (Fact Sheet #55). Washington, DC: U.S. Department of Justice.

Loucks, H. E., & Waggoner, J. E. (1999, Spring). Outreach to families. *Classroom Connections, 1*(4), 1.

Magera, D., & Wood, G. (1999). *Partnerships for at-risk learners*. http://www.educ.wsu.edu/vision/coe05.html

Magna, S. (1999). Creating a classroom culture. http://www.ispin.k12.il.us/column3.htm

Manning, M. L., & Baruth, L. G. (1995). *Students at-risk*. Boston, MA: Allyn and Bacon.

Murray, N., Kelder, S., Parcel, G., & Orphinas, P. (1998). Development of an intervention map for a parent education intervention to prevent violence among Hispanic middle school students. *Journal of School Health, 68*(2), 46–52.

National Catholic Education Association. (1993). Confronting the risks. *Momentum, 24*(2), 4.

Petersen, C. I., & Warnsby, E. (1993). Reaching disengaged parents of at-risk elementary schools. *The Education Digest, 58*(8), 22–26.

Peterson, K. D., & Deal, T. E. (1998). How leaders influence the culture of schools. *Educational Leadership, 56*(1), 28–30.

Porter, A. C., & Brophy, J. E. (1988). Synthesis of research on good teaching: Insights from the work of the Institute of Research on Teaching. *Educational Leadership, 45*(8), 74–85.

Reiff, J. C. (1996). At-risk middle level students or field dependent learners? *The Clearing House, 69*(4), 231–234.

Reiff, J. C. (1997). Multiple intelligences, culture, and equitable learning. *Childhood Education, 73*(5), 301–304.

Richardson, A. (1993). School-based teams help improve school learning environments. *Schools in the Middle, 2*(4), 26–29.

Rosenberg, P. S., Biggar, R. J., & Goedert, J. J. (1994). Declining age in HIV infections in the United States. *New England Journal of Medicine, 330*(11), 789–790.

Rossi, R. J., & Springfield, S. C. (1995). What we must do for students placed at risk. *Phi Delta Kappan, 77*(1), 73–76.

Santa, C. M., & Hoien, T. (1999). An assessment of Early Steps: A program for early intervention of reading problems. *Reading Research Quarterly, 34*(1), 54–79.

Sautter, R. C. (1995). Standing up to violence. *Phi Delta Kappan, 76*, K1–12.

Schaps, E., & Lewis, C. C. (1998). Breeding citizenship through community in school. *The Education Digest, 64*(1), 23–27.

Schmid, R. E. (1998). Three steps to self-discipline. *Teaching Exceptional Children, 30*(4), 36–39.

Schurr, S. L. (1993). Proven ways to involve parents. *The Education Digest, 58*(8), 5–8.

Schurr, S. L. (1998). Teaching, enlightening: A guide to student assessment. *Schools in the Middle, 6*(5), 22–31.

Scott, V. (1998). Breaking the cycle of incivility. *The High School Magazine, 6*(1), 4–7.

Seifert, K. L., & Hoffnung, R. J. (1991). *Child and adolescent development* (2nd ed.). Boston: Houghton-Mifflin.

Sergiovanni, T. J. (1994). *Building community in schools*. San Francisco: Jossey-Bass.

Shea, T. M., & Bauer, A. M. (1985). *Parents and teachers of exceptional children: A handbook for involvement*. Boston: Allyn and Bacon.

Silver, H., Strong, R., & Perini, M. (1997). Integrating learning styles and multiple intelligences. *Educational Leadership, 55*(1), 22–27.

Slavin, R. E. (1983). *Cooperative learning*. New York: Longman.

Slavin, R. E. (1995). *Cooperative learning: Theory, research, and practice* (2nd ed). Boston: Allyn and Bacon.

Slavin, R. E. (1996). Cooperative learning in middle and secondary schools. *The Clearing House, 69*(4), 200–204.

Spaulding, S. (1994). Four steps to effective parent involvement. *Learning, 23*(2), 36.

Sprenger, M. (1999). *Learning and memory: The brain in action*. Alexandria, VA: Association for Supervision and Curriculum Development.

Tomlinson, C. A., & Kalbfleisch, M. L. (1998). Teach me, teach my brain: A call for differentiated classrooms. *Educational Leadership 56*(3), 52–55.

U.S. Bureau of the Census. (1998). *Statistical abstracts of the United States* (118th ed.). Washington, DC: Government Printing Office.

U.S. Department of Education. (1999). *National Institute of the Education of At-Risk Students*. http://www.ed.gov/offices/OERI/At-Risk/

Vaughn, S., Bos, C. S., & Schumm, J. S. (1997). *Teaching mainstreamed, diverse, and at-risk students in the general education classroom*. Boston: Allyn and Bacon.

Walberg, H. J. (1988). Synthesis of research on time and learning. *Educational Leadership, 45*(6), 76–85.

Walker, H. M. (1998). First steps to prevent antisocial behavior. *Teaching Exceptional Children 30*(4), 16–19.

Weir, R. M. (1996). Lessons from a middle level at-risk program. *The Clearing House, 70*(1), 48–51.

Westheimer, J., & Kahne, J. (1993). Building school communities: An experience-based model. *Phi Delta Kappan, 75*(4), 324–328.

Williams, D. L., & Chavkin, N. F. (1989). Essential elements of strong parent involvement programs. *Educational Leadership, 47*(2), 18–20.

Wylie, V. L. (1992). The risk in being average. *Middle School Journal, 23*(4), 33–35.

Index

Authors

M. Lee Manning

M. Lee Manning's teaching experience includes five years with learners at-risk in the 5th, 6th, and 7th grades. He also has twenty years experience in higher education. He is currently a professor of Educational Curriculum and Instruction, Darden College of Education, Old Dominion University, in Norfolk, VA. He has approximately 155 publications in a variety of education journals such as *Childhood Education, Middle School Journal, NASSP Bulletin, American Secondary Education, Phi Delta Kappan,* and *Kappa Delta Pi Record.* His major interests include learners at-risk and multicultural education. In addition to his research and publications, he has had considerable first-hand experiences working with learners at-risk as well as their teachers. He guest-edited the March/April 1996 issue (a theme issue on at-risk students) of *The Clearing House*, a national and refereed journal.

Leroy G. Baruth

Leroy G. Baruth is a proven and respected counselor, administrator, and writer. Currently, he is professor and Department Chair in the Department of Human Development and Psychological Counseling, Reich College of Education, Appalachian State University, Boone, NC. He has published many journal articles and has authored or co-authored over 20 books. In addition to his extensive research and writing, he has worked with and counseled children at-risk in school and clinical settings. He firmly believes educators working with learners at-risk should look toward both the education and the counseling fields.